Bahau, the Elephant & the Ham

DAVID MILLER
www.dmbooks.org

Disclaimer: This book is based largely on the recollections of one woman – Sonya Miller who was 85 at the time with her brother Arthur Henry Nunes Junior providing some additional insight.

Bahau, the Elephant & the Ham is a personal reflection of the Japanese Occupation of Singapore during World War II and the journey of the Eurasian community through their eyes. Some details may have been clouded over time or differ from the memories and experiences of others.

Relevant historical information drawn from various official sources has also been included to complete the story.

Published in 2014 by DMBOOKS (Singapore) to mark the 70th anniversary of the Bahau initiative.

ISBN (Paperback): 978-981-09-0243-8
ISBN (Ebook): 978-981-09-0244-5
First edition (Ebook) – November 30 2014
First edition (Print) – December 20 2014

For more information or media enquiries, please log on to www.dmbooks.org or email admin@dmbooks.org

Copyright © David Miller, 2014

The moral right of the author has been asserted. All rights reserved. No part of this publication may be reproduced, stored in a retrieval system, or transmitted, in any form or by any means without the prior written permission of the publisher, nor be otherwise circulated in any form of binding or cover other than that in which it is published and without a similar condition being imposed on the subsequent purchaser.

Cover: The former Convent of the Holy Infant Jesus in Singapore with insert of Sonya Nunes aged 11

Cover design: DMBOOKS

Product of Singapore

in memory

ARTHUR HENRY NUNES
departed 27th March 1943   Age 43

CHARLES PERRY
departed 26TH April 1976   Age 48

MABEL NUNES
departed 31st May 1992   Age 87

DOUGLAS MILLER
departed 4th May 2009   Age 87

and for all Eurasians who perished in Bahau

I believe that even the smallest prayer will still be heard

"I had often said as we gathered under the porch in the evenings that one day soon when this terrible war was over and we were back in Singapore, we would tell our children of this time we spent in Bahau and all the things we went through but the others just scoffed at me because everyone believed that one by one, we would all die here. It was only a matter of time …"

– **Sonya Miller**
Singapore

February 2014

1

Goodbye Butterflies

I was born Sonya Mabel Nunes and in early December 1941, I was 14 years old and still a student in Standard Seven at the Raffles Girls' School. It was the year-end school vacation and Christmas was just weeks away. I was well prepared for the start of the new school term in January having already bought my books and I was eager to be reunited with all my friends.

We were living the good life, the happy life. We were not a rich family by any means but still we were content. My father was Arthur Henry Nunes and he worked in a stockbroking firm. He was a man who always walked tall with an air of complete self-assurance in his own abilities. He had an opinion on everything and would not tolerate anyone who disagreed with him. Sure he was grumpy, stubborn and hot-tempered but he was our father. He worked hard to put bread on the table and he deserved our respect.

Everything had to be done his way and on time. Three o'clock was always tea time on weekends no matter what. He would check his watch often. At four in the afternoon he would call out sternly "Four O'clock!" and no further explanation was necessary. It was bath time and dutifully my siblings and I trooped to the only bathroom patiently waiting for our turn.

My mother Mabel, who everyone in later years would call Nan, was a loving and kind woman – a woman who would and did give everything she had for her family.

Back then, there were just four kids in the family. I was the eldest followed by Arthur Henry who we all called Junior, Noreen and Kenny. Roy would come later, born during the war that was fast approaching – a war none of us thought would ever come to our door.

We were living in a house along Saint Barnabas Road near some of our relatives, the Chamrettes. These houses were built on concrete pillars which lifted them about a metre and a half off the ground.

In those days there was very little family entertainment available so all of us kids would organise plays and concerts at home. These were really big productions for us with everything planned out to the last detail including making our own costumes and stage props. I was in charge of selling tickets to relatives, friends and neighbours and would go door to door wearing a big smile and holding a bunch of tickets. These tickets were only a few cents each but inevitably someone would always ask doubtfully: "You sure you know how to sing and dance?" Critics abound I guess but these hour-long performances were all just for fun.

At home we would move aside all the furniture from the hall and this would be our stage with seats placed around it. I remember one play we performed was called *The Middle Button*. It was about a button that fell off a shirt. Junior had the role playing the missing button so he got all dressed up with a big cardboard button on his chest complete with the four holes for the thread.

My father, who never had time for such "childish nonsense", would stand by the doorway outside the house almost out of sight just to hear his eldest son proudly recite his lines.

Games were different back then; they did not cost any money and batteries were never required because we made our own fun with whatever came our way. Those were innocent and carefree times for us children.

Once while we were playing in our little garden at the back of our home, a stray duck wandered in quacking loudly to announce its presence.

"Quick, catch it. We can have it for dinner!" said my mother, a woman who never passed up on an opportunity, even a waddling one with webbed feet. We didn't have to be told twice, so with Junior and Noreen, I took off running trying to corral this noisy wayward beast of a bird. For five minutes we tried to corner it but it outsmarted us each time, never giving up the fight for its freedom and its life.

The game came to a grinding halt when we heard the shrill voice of our neighbour calling out "Di Di Di". Oh darn, – this was probably one of her ducks! We quickly darted back into the house hoping she didn't see what we were trying to do.

The field just in front of our house was our playground and together with my cousins, we used it well for every game we could imagine. I will always remember the field at the start of each new day – the sweet smell of the grass and the butterflies of every colour out to catch the last of the early morning dew.

We all knew there was a war raging in Europe but to us kids in Singapore, that war seemed like just another conflict, in a distant land, in a different time.

We were assured our island home would remain safe as it was after all labelled as Fortress Singapore. More British soldiers were arriving each week in this tiny colonial outpost of the vast empire amidst rumours of a possible Japanese invasion. British Prime Minister Winston Churchill directed two formidable warships – the *Prince of Wales* and the *Repulse* to be sent to help defend Singapore in early December.

Japan, we were told time and again, was very far away and there was no need to panic and so life here continued in a blissfully, carefree pace. How naïve we all were back then!

Everything changed for us in the early morning of December 8 1941. I was asleep and didn't hear it but at about 4am Japanese warplanes flying all the way from Saigon in Vietnam, began bombing Singapore. They struck at two British airfields in Seletar and Tengah. Some bombs also hit the city centre around Raffles Square. In all, some 70 people were killed.

At the same time up north in Malaya, thousands of Japanese soldiers led by General Tomoyuki Yamashita landed on the east coast and began advancing quickly down the peninsula heading for Singapore. Some 90 minutes after landing in Malaya, another Japanese task force attacked Pearl Harbour in Hawaii and World War II had officially begun.

The British and other Allied soldiers tried their best to halt the Japanese advance in Malaya but as we were soon to learn, they were simply outmanoeuvred and outclassed by an enemy they had always dismissed as inferior.

That very morning after the initial attack on Singapore, I watched in tears as my father along with several other men started digging in the field in front of our home. They were digging air-raid trenches and that field that we loved so much would no longer be our exclusive playground. Once beautiful and filled with wild flowers and the merry laughter of children, it was suddenly transformed into a muddy patch of barren earth with ugly holes that tore into her face. The dancing butterflies were all gone – never to return.

The innocence of my youth died that morning. Nothing would be the same ever again. Just two days later on December 10 1941 both British battleships sailing without air cover were sunk off the eastern coast of Malayan in a surprise attack by Japanese planes and with that, the fate of Singapore was sealed. There was no denying it any longer – ready or not, the war wasn't just coming – it was already here.

2

The Family Trench

There were about a dozen or more houses along Saint Barnabas Road at that time with some 100-odd residents in total. Each family built its own trench just under two metres deep. There were no sandbags so the walls were left as they were, crudely cut from the bare earth.

In our trench, my father placed a small bench for us children to sit on and to camouflage our little shelter, coconut branches were placed over the top. Looking back now, I'm sure those trenches located as they were in an open field, were plainly visible to any Japanese pilots flying by but I guess none of us thought of that at the time. We were so unprepared for this war but luckily no bombs landed anywhere close to us.

The stress of the nightly black-outs and frequent air-raid sirens took their toll, especially on the adults. They seemed grumpy and on edge all the time but things were different for us kids. Schools, we were told, would remain closed indefinitely and so chores aside, we were quite free to pass the time any way we wanted. Besides the four of us, there were also my other cousins Margie, Maisie and Henry to play with.

Our little ragtag gang would still sneak out to play in the field with the other kids from the neighbourhood when no one was watching. Sometimes a careless child would fall into one of the trenches but no one was ever hurt.

Over the next two weeks, those mournful sirens would go off many times especially at night. We would each grab our pillows and follow our parents out. Huddling in the trench was a new adventure of sorts. I remember Kenny, the youngest of our brood, would soon get bored with all the waiting and he would start digging the sides of the trench with a stick. Soon clumps of earth would be falling on him followed by the inevitable scolding from Mum.

Most of the early air-raid warnings proved to be false alarms and after a while Junior was tired with the nightly ritual of heading for cover. While the rest of us ran for the family trench, he would sneak back home and crawl into his bed.

The sporadic bombings at night soon increased with frequent daylight attacks on Singapore. Things were now getting more serious and more dangerous. When those sirens went off, it only took one yell from my father to send us scurrying like meek little mice to the relative safety of our little trench.

My mother would grab her figurine of Saint Francis along with a few other favourite saints before following us and there, kneeling in the trench with an armful of statues clutched tightly to her chest, she would be praying aloud trying to invoke divine protection for her family and all the others in that little field.

For us children these air raids were both scary and exciting. Crouched in our trench we would be straining our ears to pick up the first sounds of the approaching bombers. Then we would hear the planes flying overhead – all of them heading towards the city centre just a few kilometres away. Sometimes through the coconut branches we would catch a fleeting glimpse, just tiny black dots really, as the planes flew by. Soon there would be sounds of muffled explosions in the distance as the bombs found their targets time and again.

In the early days of these raids Mum would tell us of seeing British fighters flying up to meet the attacking Japanese squadrons and of the aerial duels that followed; but soon there would be no more British fighter planes left. They had all been destroyed and the Japanese were now free to attack us at will.

Like many young men, my father was part of the volunteer Local Defence Corps and was issued with a very ancient-looking rifle. During the air raids, he would position himself a distance from our trench and start shooting at the planes as they soared just below the clouds.

Between the deafening gunshots, he would be screaming curses and more at the Japanese pilots. Shaking his fist to the sky he would yell out: "I'm going to kill those buggers!" along with other colourful language that I am not allowed to repeat! My mother would be begging him to get inside the trench for his own safety. She would try in vain to reason with him that the planes were far out of range but his temper knew no bounds.

I guess it is difficult now to comprehend the sheer horror of those days and the desolate vulnerability we all felt. There was very little we could do to protect ourselves – usually it was just blind fate that determined who lived and who died.

One of our neighbours was an elderly French woman who was probably more than a little senile. When the air-raid sirens would start wailing, she would take a chair and sit in her garden with a handkerchief on her head.

I had the chance to talk to her one day and I asked her why she did that. She told me the handkerchief was there in case it rains! Maybe she simply could not comprehend that war had arrived and everything we knew of our old lives had changed. I never knew what happened to her but I hope she made it.

No one told us kids much about what was going on with the war but I realised things must have been very grim. The inescapable facts were that the Japanese were now in Malaya and they were fighting their way quickly towards Singapore.

The Malayan capital of Kuala Lumpur, abandoned by the retreating British forces, was captured on January 11 1942 and by the end of the month, the Allies had all been pushed back to Singapore.

There were newspaper reports of many civilians killed in the fighting up north and of rampant looting by the Japanese soldiers as they overran villages, towns and cities.

The Causeway, the only land bridge to Malaya, was blown up on January 31 to try and slow down the Japanese onslaught towards Singapore. By now, we all knew the inevitable was coming and we were completely on our own.

Like some families, we attempted to flee the country and escape the land war that was surely heading our way. We heard there were ships leaving for Australia that would take civilian refugees to safety. 'Civilian refugees' – we never thought of ourselves as that – until now.

No payment was needed to board these ships so Mum hastily got us to pack our things. Each person was restricted to just one bag. It was very much a spur of the moment decision with little thought paid to the real dangers we may face in the hostile open ocean where there would be no place to hide. If everything went well, it would take a week at least to reach the western coast of Australia.

One of our neighbours, a teacher at Saint Joseph's Institution, said he would drive us to the dock but then something happened in his school on the day we were supposed to leave and he couldn't get away to take us to the ship.

Left with no other options, we decided to walk, bags and all. Unfortunately, or fortunately as it turned out, we arrived there too late and our ship had already left. Some days later we heard that it was bombed and sank at sea. I'm not sure if anyone survived. The rumour at the time was that the unarmed vessel went down with everyone on board.

3

To The Convent

By early February, the situation was looking increasing bleak. The Imperial Japanese Army had breached Singapore's northern defences and columns of troops were steadily advancing south to the city.

One of our relatives, Auntie Inda, suggested that Mum take her children and seek refuge in the convent along with many other Eurasian families who were already heading there.

There would be safety in numbers, she advised. If the British were forced to surrender, which was now a possibility that could no longer be ignored, Eurasians being the closest community to them may soon bear the brunt of reprisals by the Japanese.

Meanwhile British and other foreign nationals were being hastily evacuated from Singapore but locals like us were now excluded from these last lifeboats to safety. On February 12 1942 with little choice, Mum again had us pack our bags and we set off to the Convent of the Holy Infant Jesus in Victoria Street.

Only females and young children were allowed to stay at the convent so my brother Junior who was 12 years old and my cousin Henry had to stay at Victoria School which catered to boys of their age. This school was also designated as a treatment centre for civilian casualties and one of my aunts, Molly, who was a volunteer helping to run the canteen, went with them.

When we reached the convent which was located close to the city centre, we were confronted with a most chaotic and distressing scene with more Eurasian families arriving by the minute. Under any other circumstances, it would have been a noisy and joyous clan reunion but this was different. The mood was subdued and looking at the mothers trying to herd their children into the queue, you could almost see the fear and desperation in their eyes. No one knew what to expect but the nuns did their best to calm everyone down and get our temporary living arrangements sorted out as best they could. As the school within the walled convent grounds was closed, we were told to settle ourselves in any of the empty classrooms.

We decided to take one on the top floor thinking it may be safer but time would prove that decision to be almost fatal.

The classrooms back then were quite big as they had to accommodate up to about 40 children so there was much room to spare. We shared ours with the Mowe and the Paulo families.

Although the nuns already had several orphaned children and babies to look after, they still tried to help us as much as they could.

There must have been over 200 people seeking refuge inside the convent yet somehow the nuns managed to feed everyone with their meagre supplies and even collected water in large jars so that we could all bathe. They selflessly gave up their mattresses so that the children at least could have a comfortable place to sleep and I for one will never forget their kindness during such a difficult time.

For us kids, roaming around the convent grounds and its many buildings brought new adventures. Most of us knew the layout well as we had visited the school many times before but there still were lots of dark nooks and crannies for us to explore which kept us occupied and for the most part, out of trouble.

One afternoon just a day or two after we arrived at the convent, my mother decided to give Kenny, the youngest one, his daily bath. She took him down to the bathrooms on the ground floor as Noreen and I went to play with some of our cousins. A few minutes later, without any warning, the Japanese began shelling the city again.

One small artillery round tore through the roof of the building just above our classroom and exploded. The shell didn't do much structural damage as I recall but poor Mrs Paulo, who was resting in the room at the time, was killed probably by the concussion of the blast.

At that time, my father was staying at a friend's house near Capitol Cinema just across the road from the convent so he could keep an eye on us while he performed his military duties. His small room overlooked the convent grounds and he knew exactly which classroom we were camping in.

When he saw that it had taken a direct hit from the artillery shell with smoke still billowing from what remained of the roof, he came running to check if we were okay. I had never seen my father look so worried before but I guess he was expecting the worst. In his haste he ran right past me without even noticing.

A large part of the roof had caved in littering the ground with debris and he must have seen Mrs Paulo's body lying there partially buried. Hysterically my father began digging with his bare hands through the burning rubble thinking that his family was trapped or worse.

A nun soon came by and gently tapped him on his shoulder. "Don't dig," she said calmly, "they are not there." Only then did he notice the rest of us standing outside along the corridor still in shock. Whilst we were all shaken by the attack, I don't think it actually dawned on us children how lucky we were simply to be alive.

Following the attack, Mum moved us to another classroom on the ground floor. Now every time the sirens went off, we all had to remain together in one of a few classrooms which were designated as communal shelters.

In the days that followed, the convent was struck by bombs from planes and artillery shells eight times with one narrowly missing its beautiful chapel. I was told that several civilians, injured in some of these attacks on Singapore, were being treated at the convent but that was in a different part of the building which was off limits to us children.

We all knew the end was drawing near. Our taps went dry as bombs ruptured the underground pipes. There was no electricity and we were practically out of food. Soon there were rumours that the British were about to surrender. It was bitterly apparent to everyone that despite their earlier confidence about stopping the Japanese advance, the British army was simply overwhelmed and could not hold out much longer.

The most formidable weapons which the British had were five 15-inch guns located on Singapore's east and south coasts. Built in 1939, they were designed to deter a seaborne invasion and to protect the city centre and its nearby harbour. The British had assumed wrongly that the Japanese would not attack from the north through the thick and seemingly impenetrable Malayan jungle. While these guns could be turned to aim northwards, their armour-piercing ammunition which was more suited for attacks against battleships did little to stop the land invasion through Malaya. Many of the shells simply failed to detonate in the soft jungle ground. These guns, the largest deployed outside Britain during the war, were destroyed on February 12 1942 to prevent them from falling into enemy hands.

The general feeling at the time was that surrender would be a better option because many more civilians would surely be killed if the fighting got any closer to the city. Still there were other rumours floating around that the Japanese in an act of vengeance would slaughter all Eurasians, children included.

The surrender took place on February 15 1942 just three days after we arrived at the convent. We all listened intently to the announcement on the radio with rising fear and anxiety.

A day or two after the surrender we heard that a large group of British and Australian troops were being marched through the city by Japanese guards to Changi Prison where they would begin their internment as prisoners of war. I'm not sure if they actually passed by the convent because Mum forbade us from looking out the windows.

4

We Are Now Your Masters

Soon we were told that some Japanese soldiers were on their way to the convent. We all had to get dressed up and gather in the convent's gallery for an inspection. Sitting on the steps where school assemblies used to be held each morning, the nuns reminded us to stand up smartly and bow as soon as these 'important guests' arrived.

No one really knew what to expect and they made all the children sit in the front row.

Perhaps someone thought the sight of so many little ones, all looking a little sweaty and dishevelled as we always were, might invoke some sympathy from the Japanese.

I can still vividly remember the moment the Japanese walked into that hall, and into our lives. There were a few officers in their dirty uniforms with long swords hanging from their belts. Accompanying the soldiers were several local civilians one of whom was a rather plump woman, carrying the Japanese flag. This was the first real Japanese flag that I had ever seen but soon such flags would be flying all over Singapore.

The officer in charge gave a long speech in Japanese and an interpreter translated it to us as we gathered there in stunned silence. We all kept our heads bowed and prayed that we would not be shot as the minutes ticked by. I can't remember everything the man said but one line stuck in my head even after all these years – "We are now your masters …"

That was a stark and ominous statement which spoke volumes for not only were the Japanese in charge of us now, they saw themselves as being better than everyone else – a class apart and a superior race – with the right to decide between life or death at will.

We stayed on at the convent for nine more days after the surrender but we knew it was only a temporary measure. While they appeared menacing, it did not seem that the Japanese were about to slaughter all the Eurasians as we once feared. The nuns could no longer afford to feed us and life needed to go on so we had to leave the relative safety of our convent sanctuary and get on with our lives as best we could. No one doubted that the coming days, weeks, months and years were going to be very different from anything we could possibly even imagine.

We moved out of the convent and returned to our home in Saint Barnabas Road. Junior soon rejoined us and we were a family once again but the future remained far from certain.

Like the rest of us, Junior too had his share of stories to relate about his close shaves with death. While taking refuge in Victoria School with our cousin Henry, the boys would often go out to the school field. Just beyond the fence, the British had positioned an anti-aircraft battery manned by about half a dozen soldiers.

"Being young boys, we would go to the fence every chance we had just to talk to the soldiers. They were really friendly showing us their weapons and telling us stories about the action they had seen. Once while we were chatting, the sirens suddenly went off. The soldiers immediately shouted at us to get back to the school and take cover. Running back to the building, we could hear the enemy planes diving in as the British gunners opened fire.

"The explosions that followed were deafening and they shook the ground. When it was over, Henry and I went out again to see if the soldiers were okay. Their gunpost must have taken several direct hits. All we saw was a big smouldering hole in ground and bits of flesh still dripping blood were hanging on the school fence. The soldiers, they were all dead – every single one of them," recalled Junior.

I remember another incident that happened soon after the Japanese took over the island. All adult Eurasians were ordered to assemble at the Padang – a national field in the heart of the city, to be screened by some military officers.

In no uncertain terms our small and vulnerable community was warned to cooperate fully with our new overlords or else. Luckily nothing untoward happened that day and soon everyone was allowed to return home.

The local newspapers which were all taken over by the Japanese would often print stories about the Eurasian community in Singapore accusing us of being trouble-makers and warning us of serious repercussions if we did not cooperate with the Japanese military. This was all just propaganda of course and the simple truth was that we, like everyone else, were simply trying to get by each day.

While their distrust of Eurasians was obvious, it was the large Chinese community in Singapore that bore the brunt of Japanese cruelty. The Imperial Japanese Army believed that many of the local Chinese supported China in the Second Sino-Japanese War through a series of fund-raising propagandist events. Hundreds of young men were hastily screened and taken away, never to be seen again. There were rumours of mass executions but at that time, no one really knew the truth. However these brutal killings proved to be hauntingly real and many – some estimates put the number at 50,000 or more – were lined up and shot along the shore at Changi Beach and at other places in what were to be called the Sook Ching massacres. The term Sook Ching literally means to 'purge through cleansing'.

Many bodies simply washed out to sea while others were hastily buried in large and unmarked graves. This genocide would remain a painful but closed chapter for two decades until 1962 when several of these mass graves were unearthed across the island in Siglap, Bukit Timah and Changi. The remains were collected and placed in large urns to be interred at a new landmark in Singapore – the Civilian War Memorial. Now every year on February 15, the anniversary of the Fall of Singapore, air-raid sirens would once again sound across the island as a poignant reminder of these mass murders that have never been avenged.

5
Life in *Syonan-to*

In an instant or so it seemed, many things changed following the surrender of Singapore. The island was now called *Syonan-to*, meaning 'Light of the South'. To the Chinese, *Syonan-to* sounded much like 'Birdcage Island' in the local Hokkien dialect – certainly not a good omen.

The year was no longer 1942 but rather 2602 according to the Japanese calendar. Clocks were reset to Tokyo time. The Japanese Emperor Hirohito was to be revered as a God and bowing to the north-east every morning towards the Imperial Palace in the Japanese capital which now did not seem so far away, was a ritual we all gradually got used to.

Schools were eventually reopened and everyone, especially the children, had to learn Japanese. All textbooks were printed in Japanese and we had to sing with gusto the Nippon anthem.

I guess most people assumed back then that this was not just a temporary phase of life but the start of a new cold reality which we simply had to accept for better or for worse.

In the cinemas, only Japanese movies and propaganda films were shown. The English and Chinese newspapers here had very little local news and a lot of misinformation on the success of the Japanese military actions overseas.

I remember reading the many 'MAD' notices run by the Military Administration Department in the newspaper every day. One notice run daily would carry a long list of basic necessities such as rice, assorted vegetables, chickens, ducks, prawns and a variety of local fish. It would detail the maximum price these could be sold for to prevent shopkeepers from jacking up prices. Other notices would order fishermen for example to return to work immediately, while doctors were reminded to report all cases of dysentery on the island. Sometimes you would get an unusual notice. One asked for information on a missing Japanese aircraft that apparently disappeared during an attack on Singapore. MAD promised a reward for information leading to its recovery. Each day the newspaper also ran a column called *'Nippon-Go Lessons'*. These taught the people basic Japanese phrases.

Local radio stations were also taken over by the military and listening to foreign news bulletins was an offence punishable by death. I remember one story that made its rounds in whispered rumours was of a man who was caught listening to the BBC radio service. The *Kempeitai* – the Japanese secret police – put a pencil in each ear and then slammed these into his head. No one knew how true stories like these were but the effects on all of us, children as well as adults, were chilling.

Although I did not see this myself, many others said they saw several decapitated human heads displayed on poles along bridges near the Cathay Cinema and in front of the YMCA building along Stamford Road which was the headquarters of the *Kempeitai*.

While it was nearly impossible to get accurate information on what was happening beyond the island, we did hear of some rumours which were trickling out of Malaya. These stories included one concerning a massacre of Eurasians living in Johore at the Ulu Tiram estate. From what we were told, many Eurasian civilians – women and children included – were rounded up. With their hands tied behind their backs, they were bayoneted and their bodies were dumped into a shallow trench which the men had been forced to dig earlier.

After Singapore's surrender, we often saw groups of British and Australian soldiers who were put to work repairing the streets near our home in Saint Barnabas Road. They worked under the blazing sun watched closely by the Japanese guards. Hot, sweaty and apparently starving, these POWs would stop and wave when they saw us kids playing nearby. We would return the big smiles and wave back enthusiastically. Sometimes, when my mother was around, she would tell us to go and give them some bananas or a bottle of water. We would run out and give the guards and their prisoners handfuls of the fruit or a cool drink whenever we had any to spare.

I can still see the look on their faces – for a brief moment, these prisoners would be happy and so would we. The only reason we gave some refreshments to the guards first was to appease them so they wouldn't stop us from doing the same with their prisoners. Those poor chaps – they all looked so thin and hungry.

The hardest part for all of us was just getting by with the daily necessities of life. We soon had another mouth to feed when Roy, my youngest brother, was born on September 14 1942.

Everything was so expensive especially food. The Japanese issued their official currency which everyone called banana money because these notes carried an image of a banana plant on the front. These notes were basically worthless but still for most of us, this new currency was always in short supply. You could still buy things on the black market using the now rare Straits Settlements money if you had any left and knew where to go. There were of course some very wealthy Eurasians around but we certainly weren't one of them.

Sweet potatoes and yams became the staple food for most people because these were cheaper than rice and could be grown quite easily even in small backyard gardens. To add some variety to the daily diet, inventive ways of cooking and preparing tapioca soon became the fashion.

This was precisely what the Japanese encouraged people to do, to grow their own food even as they began issuing food ration cards. Just about every available space was soon converted into little vegetable gardens.

The front lawn of schools like Saint Joseph's Institution in Bras Basah Road where in years to come my sons would attend, were ploughed by hand and planted with an assortment of vegetables. The same thing happened with our national field, the Padang. Men were forced under the watchful eye of Japanese guards to tend to large communal farms.

It was this critical shortage of food that triggered the next chapter of our lives under the Japanese Occupation, but more on this later.

We lived in perpetual fear, not just of the unpredictable Japanese soldiers who patrolled the streets, but we were also afraid for my father. Even after the surrender, he did not change his ways. He would curse the 'little dirty Japanese scum' – although thankfully not to their faces – every chance he had. We were all afraid that one day he would be caught and may literally lose his head.

My father had contracted tuberculosis, a very common and often fatal illness in those days. As he lay delirious and dying in bed at home, I can still remember him saying that he could see angels by the window and Jesus standing nearby waiting to take him home. One of our more distant relatives (and I shall not say who this was) would mutter under her breath that with the grumpy life he lived, he would probably be heading in the opposite direction! That was so mean.

Dad passed away on the March 27 1943 and was buried at the Bidadari cemetery. I remember that he had a very nice headstone complete with a glass urn containing fresh flowers. He was only 43 years old and like so many others, he was much too young to die.

After Dad's passing, we moved again, this time we stayed with one of Mum's relatives and her family as we could not afford to pay the rent on our home.

Life was even tougher now without a breadwinner and with five young mouths to feed, food and money were always in short supply for my poor Mum.

In their dining room there was a big table for our relatives and a little round one in the corner for Mum and the five of us. I guess survival instincts even among blood relatives kick in when you can never be sure where or when your next meal was coming from. We were told not to touch their food of which there always seemed to be plenty, or hang around their table when they were eating.

Mum would always tell us to remain in our room when the relatives were having their meals. But Roy who was barely a toddler would sometimes sneak out and make his way to their dinner table, probably because he was just curious as to what was going on. He and Mum were always getting scolded for such little things. Sigh – it was all so sad.

Even the guava tree in their garden was off limits to us. Our relative would count the fruits still on the tree and if even one was missing, there would be hell to pay. We were often accused of stealing the fruits but truth be told, as hungry as we were, we never touched a single one.

To make ends meet, Noreen, Junior and I had to stop our studies and get jobs. Playing games in the field was now a distant but happy memory as circumstances forced us to grow up quickly. Noreen and I worked as salesgirls whilst Junior got a job disinfecting drains to stem the breeding of mosquitoes.

Mum too began working in a shop along Orchard Road which sold a wide range of basic necessities exclusively for the Japanese soldiers. Whenever she could, Mum would steal anything from work that she could get her hands on. I remember I soon found our little pantry cupboard suddenly filled with many cans of corned beef.

In those dark times, primitive hunger overrode morality and despite the mortal dangers, you did what you had to do to survive and feed your family. Mum would say stealing under such circumstances was a 'white sin' and God would forgive her. I have absolutely no doubts about that.

I worked at Whiteaways Department Store which the Japanese had renamed as *Gun Shu*

Ho. It was in the heart of the city where Maybank Towers stands today. I sold mostly toiletries such as soap, toothbrushes and Japanese underwear for a monthly salary of just $30.

While there was an open lorry that we could hop on to take us from our home in Thomson Road to town, it was always full and clambering onto a lorry in a dress was no easy feat. So Mum, Noreen and I opted to walk instead.

Our route took us past a polluted canal and a veterinary hospital along Kampong Java Road. There was a Japanese shrine nearby where a soldier was killed. As we walked by, we had to stop and bow before the shrine even if no Japanese soldiers appeared to be in sight. It was always better to be safe than sorry.

Our daily walk to work would take us past a small cemetery near the Kandang Kerbau Hospital (Kandang Kerbau literally means "buffalo shed" in Malay). It would be in this hospital where in later years my nine children would all be born.

There was a big hole in the fence around the Istana – once the seat of government in the 'old' Singapore. We would cut through the Istana grounds and this shortcut would take us to Orchard Road where Mum worked. From there, Noreen and I would walk a little further to get to our store.

I quickly adapted to the pace of working life which was interesting and most of the girls working there were Eurasians. Our supervisor was an elderly Japanese woman who we called *Mama-san*. I remember we would always be in fits of laughter and calling out frantically for *Mama-san* every time we had some old Japanese women who needed help trying on the underwear before buying. *Mama-san* seemed quite fond of us girls and would often ask us to teach her some English so she could converse with the local customers.

Still it was a time of war and there were shortages of practically everything. As salesgirls, we all stole whatever we could get away with. Since I worked selling toiletries, I took as much soap and toothbrushes that I could safely smuggle out. These would be worth their weight in gold to us in just a few months.

But you had to be very careful when you were flicking something. I remember one of the salesgirls was caught stealing and the Japanese civilians who were running the shop tied her to a pole outside near what was then the General Post Office (now Fullerton Hotel). I am not sure how long she remained there humiliated as hundreds of people walked past pretending not to notice. I felt it was so wicked of them to do that but I guess they wanted to make her an example to the rest of us. It worked well at least for a few days and then we were back to pilfering whatever we could get away with.

Life was pleasant in some ways and we used to have dance parties quite often usually at the Conceicao house near the hospital. It was at one of these parties that I met my future husband Douglas Miller. He was a dashing young man with his swept-back hair and the top button of his shirt was always undone.

I had seen him often but at that time, we were just very casual friends. I remember once we were all at a party and everyone was having a good time. When it was over and Douglas was walking home, he fell into a large drain just outside the house. He was wearing a white suit and was apparently covered in mud!

When we girls heard about it, we all laughed so much thinking it was simply hilarious. Still a bunch of us thought we should at least check in on him and see if he was okay but in truth, many of us just wanted to see what became of his white suit.

He was staying with his family in Mackenzie Road just a short distance away. When we got there, Douglas being the only son was being fussed over by his mother and sisters. I remember his mother giving me a stern look when she saw me among the other girls followed by the complete 'once-over'. Sometime later I heard from mutual friends that Douglas had told his family that I was his girlfriend.

In the months that followed, I got to know him better. We talked often about this terrible war and all the things we had seen and heard. Douglas had a government job in town and he confirmed that rumour about those decapitated heads displayed on poles. He saw it for himself one day while on his way to work and said he would never forget that sickening sight for as long as he lived. I was just glad that I was spared of having to keep that horrifying memory with me all these years.

6
The Night Train to Bahau

Towards the end of 1943 with food in Singapore running desperately short, the Japanese came up with a plan to lessen the demand by simply moving some people out from the island.

Malaya, outside its cities and towns, held vast sparsely populated lands. A large group of Chinese from Singapore formed the first band of refugees to be resettled in a remote jungle area called Endau in Johore. Each family was given a piece of land to live on, farm and feed themselves with little supervision from the Japanese or so they were led to believe. Excess produce from these farms was supposed to be brought back to Singapore to help feed the local population.

The Japanese in their typical propaganda hailed this experiment as a 'gigantic success' and soon another similar initiative was planned near the small Malayan town of Bahau in the state of Negri Sembilan. This would be mainly for Catholic Eurasians and neutrals such as the Swiss and Danes along with a few Catholic Chinese. I don't really know why the Catholic community was singled out.

The Japanese Command sought the cooperation of Bishop Adrian Devals of the Catholic Church in Singapore. In a private meeting with the bishop, the Japanese had apparently hinted that should the Eurasian community reject this 'generous offer', it may be subjected to more swoops by agents of the *Kempeitai* who were always on the lookout for British sympathisers and Eurasians were naturally among their prime suspects. They also warned that Eurasian men may be sent to work on the dreaded Burma Railway which was soon to be called the Death Railway. Stretching over 400 kilometres between Bangkok, Thailand, and Rangoon in Burma, it was said that on average, one person died for every sleeper that was laid.

Still, going to Bahau was voluntary and the option to stay or go split the community. Going there and being away from the oppressive Japanese rule in Singapore seemed like a good idea at the time although it was fraught with uncertainty. Food was another major push factor. Many reasoned that if the Chinese could do it, so could we. But the Chinese survived because they were hardworking and resourceful. For Eurasians, many of whom had known only sedentary white-collar work it would be an entirely different kettle of fish.

The newspapers began running daily stories encouraging Eurasians to take up this offer, promising that Bahau would be a "little paradise" and I guess many of us bought into that lie. If nothing else, Bahau seemed to offer a faint glimmer of hope in such desperate and hungry times.

The Japanese went to great lengths to get Eurasians to support the Bahau initiative, reasoning that it would be in their best interest. We would be living out in the country on large farms and all we had to do was to feed ourselves and we could even make good money selling any excess produce that we grew. Land would be given to us along with farming tools and seeds to get us started. The Japanese even assured the community that Bahau was free of that dreaded jungle disease, malaria.

At that time, we were staying with some of my mother's relatives the Perry's and after much discussion, they had decided to go. Left with little choice, Mum and the five of us children had to follow.

We would all be leaving Singapore forever or so we thought. Everything we had was to be sorted and packed and in a way we were quite excited about the move. Many families decided to take some luxuries with them including pianos and even an organ. Pets too would be included in the big Eurasian exodus.

Looking back, I don't think many Eurasians fully realised just how difficult and downright primitive the life in Bahau would be, even though it was just a few hours away by train.

Over the next week we began packing up as best we could. Thanks to my 'inventive efforts' at work, we were well stocked in the soap and toothbrushes department, enough to last us a lifetime or so it seemed. Mum too boxed up lots of sheets, tablecloths and curtains along with all our clothes and of course her secret food cache – the tins of liberated corned beef. She had also bought a large leg of cured ham still packed in corn husk. It was a major financial investment for the time but that single leg of ham would be more useful than we could ever imagine.

I wasn't sure what to make of our impending move to Bahau but it didn't seem like we had much choice. However, we would be going there with our extended family and those numbers would soon make the difference between life and death.

In heading to Bahau, I would be leaving my boyfriend Douglas behind. He promised to try and join us in a few months after we had settled in. It must have been a very difficult choice for him to make as his family would still be in Singapore but it was his decision.

Already three batches of Eurasians had made the move to Bahau. The first group consisting mainly of young single men went up in late December 1943 just after Christmas. They would help to prepare the settlement and clear as much land as possible before the rest of the clan arrived.

In February 1944 it was our turn to go. The elders of the community, people like Bishop Devals and Dr Charles Paglar, a surgeon who was coerced to serve as the president of the Japanese-sponsored Eurasian Welfare Association, spoke at length to the families who had agreed to head north.

They explained the realities of the Bahau initiative. It was not going to be a bed of roses by any stretch of the imagination but it would be a chance to start life again on free land away from our Japanese overlords. Families who opted to take up this offer would also be given some cash to help them get started but the rest would be up to us. It was to be a leap of faith, or more likely, a plunge into the unknown.

On February 14th 1944 – Valentine's Day, we set off to begin a new and uncertain chapter of our lives. It was almost two years to the day since the surrender of Singapore.

We were told to assemble on the grounds of the Good Shepherd Cathedral with all our belongings. From there, buses took us to the train station at Tanjong Pagar.

It was already dark when the train that would take us north finally pulled out of the station. We were all packed in like sardines with barely enough seats to go around. Luckily Mum had one as she was carrying my youngest brother Roy who was only seventeen months old at the time.

Like most of the other youngsters, I stood up the whole way. It was a long journey, some five hours, but we were all excited and nervous at the same time. I expected some Japanese soldiers to be on the train guarding our group but I did not see any around. Maybe they were keeping their promise to leave us to ourselves and that could only be a good thing.

There were a few Chinese families on the train but the majority of the passengers were Eurasians like us, fleeing for our lives and hoping for the best. There were also several nuns accompanying our group and for some reason, just their presence amongst us was very reassuring. After all, the nuns had taken good care of my family when we stayed at the convent and I hoped they would continue to do the same.

The mood was light and many of the boys soon had their guitars out. We sang into the night as the old train continued churning along its tracks, leaving Singapore and the only life I had known further and further behind in the darkness. Maybe Bahau would not be that bad after all. I had my fingers crossed.

7

Floating Pork!

After several long stops, it was dawn and still dark when we finally reached our destination. Arriving in Bahau was just as chaotic a scene as when we had left Singapore. It was a lot of 'hurry up and wait'. All this was made worse for us when we discovered that Kenny, who had been playing with some of the other children earlier, had lost one of his shoes on the train. As people were busy gathering their things to leave the carriage, I was on my hands and knees trying to locate that missing shoe. I eventually found it and soon we too had all our bags unloaded.

Our settlement located deep in the jungle, was still eight long kilometres away from Bahau town. Lorries were arranged to take us the rest of the way to our new home which was called *Fuji-go* meaning Fuji Village after the sacred Japanese mountain.

However the dirt road to our settlement was mired in thick mud and after just three kilometres, the vehicles could go no further. We had to walk the remaining five kilometres carrying all our worldly possessions. Luckily we were able to hire a bullock cart for Mum who was carrying Roy and we loaded our little mountain of belongings onto it.

The land around Bahau was very hilly and we were constantly going up the side of one hill and down the other. As the eldest, it was my responsibility to keep the rest of the kids together and I kept a special eye on Kenny making sure he didn't lose another shoe along the way!

On both sides of the dirt road stood the dark and imposing Malayan jungle and we could hear the calls of monkeys in the distance hidden by the thick canopy. We were told that herds of wild elephants were living there along with deer, wild boars and snakes of all description. Even the odd tiger or two was said to roam between the vine-covered trees. It seemed to me that we weren't just travelling down a little country road but we were going back in time as well and suddenly the bright lights of Singapore felt so very far away.

I'm not sure how long it took us to walk those last kilometres but we finally made it to *Fuji-go*. It was really in the middle of nowhere and the tiny crude settlement with its rough timber huts and thatched roofs was an extremely depressing sight. This was far from the rosy picture of country bliss that the Japanese had painted.

At the centre of this little refugee village was the administrative office. There was a small sentry outpost that housed a few Japanese soldiers but they never bothered us much. One cluster of buildings was designated as a convent for the nuns and another was home for the Catholic brothers and priests. There was even a small clinic. I didn't notice it then but there was an open area just behind the clinic. This empty plot of land was reserved as a cemetery and it would soon be filled with little white crosses.

Locals from Bahau and Kuala Pilah, another town further away, were there to greet us or so I thought. Many had parked their old cars and rusty pick-up trucks by the side of the road ready to sell vegetables, chickens and just about anything else one might need.

While they seemed friendly enough, I wondered what they really thought of us. Behind the broad smiles, I'm sure they felt that none of us refugees from the big city down south, were ready to face the challenges of surviving out here in this desolate wilderness.

Maybe they just saw us as an economic opportunity – the chance to make a quick buck or two and who could really blame them? Everyone was struggling just to get by and our struggle had barely begun.

We were moved into communal long houses called *bangsals* which would be our temporary accommodation until we were processed. We also had to wait for our house to be built on the plot of land that we had been given.

Uncle Orgie, the family patriarch at the time, had already made arrangements with some local Chinese carpenters from the village to build our new home. Work had been underway for some weeks and the wooden house was almost completed by the time we arrived in Bahau.

He would not be staying with us as he held a good job in Singapore. Still in the months to come, Uncle Orgie would visit us often bringing up some much-needed food, crop seeds and cash to keep us going. He was in essence, our only lifeline to the outside world.

Just like the situation on the train, the longhouses were packed with people and you had to sleep head to head with total strangers. Each longhouse could take about 50 people.

Like other families, we arranged our bags around us to form a mini-wall of sorts, guarding the precious little space we each had. With so many young boys around, Mum made sure us girls, my sister Noreen and I, stayed well protected in the middle of the family huddle as we slept at night.

One of our neighbours in the longhouse was a very nice family, the Oehlers. He was a dentist and they had a baby with them along with their two pet dogs which were well-behaved. Despite the cramped conditions, everyone tried to get along as best they could. I remember one of the young boys there was called Andrew Deans and he helped us out running little errands for Mum.

With the longhouses packed so tightly, there was no room for families to prepare and cook their own meals so food was provided by the Japanese. At mealtimes we would sit in rows while someone would dish out some food on our plates. It was mostly rice in watery soup and if you were lucky, you had a little bit of pork thrown in. It was really just a thin slice of meat attached to a thick glob of tasteless fat.

Someone would inevitably yell out: 'Eh! Floating pork' and we would all laugh. It seemed quite funny at the time but little did we realise then that any form of meat, even 'floating pork', was soon to be a luxury.

Rainwater collected in large hand-dug ditches was all we had for bathing. Whilst *Fuji-go* did have some wells with clear water, these were used strictly for drinking.

Junior told us about an amusing encounter he had heard regarding the drinking wells in our little village. "No one enjoyed bathing in muddy water because you end up feeling even dirtier than when you started. There was one chap, Roland Cornelius, who decided one night to use the water from a well outside the home for the brothers and priests. With no one around, he stripped down and was happily soaping himself when of all people, the bishop himself walked by. Roland kept bowing to the bishop and apologising profusely while trying to cover himself at the same time. Still he got a ticking off from the bishop for wasting precious drinking water!"

Thankfully we didn't have to stay in the longhouse for very long as it was only about a week or so after we arrived that our house was ready. We were about to get the first glimpse of our new home and I couldn't wait to settle into somewhere more permanent.

From the centre of *Fuji-go*, it was another 15 minute walk to our plot of land and then we were finally home at last!

8

Starting Over

We were really quite lucky as the plot of land that we were given was not only relatively close to the village but it also had a stream running through it which provided us with a ready source of water. It was quite a large stream about five metres across but rather shallow at about waist-deep. There were even a few small fish in the stream and the water seemed clean enough.

One of the first decisions we made was that no one was allowed to bathe in the stream or worse still, use it as a toilet as we wanted to keep the water as clean as possible. We could only hope that families living further upstream were doing the same.

Our plot also had a well from which we could draw groundwater and this provided some amusement for us in the months to come. In the dry season when you threw a bucket in, you were more than likely to end up with just a frog in it!

The presence of that stream did cause some tension among those staying in Bahau and we were lucky indeed to have it running through our land. Other people without a stream or a well in their backyard, would have to walk a long distance to get their daily supply of water and they would need lots of it for the crops which they intended to grow.

As for our plot, it was big, really big, about three acres of semi-cleared land along with about two acres of jungle. There was a little driveway of sorts leading from the road to our house however a big tree had fallen across this dirt track. Someone said it was a bad omen to leave the tree there but it was just too large to move without heavy equipment and of course we didn't have any. Still the old tree provided us with a ready source of firewood but it took a lot of hard work, back-breaking work really, to chop off the branches using nothing but an old hand axe.

I think that when you are young, everything seems so much larger and our house, well it looked huge to me! It was capped with an *attap* roof, had three large bedrooms and one smaller one with a balcony running its entire length. The wood was still green and rough, having been cut from trees in the surrounding jungle just weeks earlier.

Mum and the five of us had a room to ourselves. We would soon add a small extension for Junior. The others in the house at the time were the Perry's – Auntie Josephine (the wife of Uncle Orgie), Reggie, Moe, Charlie and Gwen. Yes almost everyone in those days had their names shortened for some reason. We also had a few of Reggie's friends from Singapore join us.

Just across the road were more relatives – Ivy and Edmund. They had so much more land than the two of them could ever farm on their own so they rented part of it to an old Indian couple. Until today I can't recall why, but we all called the couple Diddle and the Fiddle!

Next to Ivy's plot stayed the Bogaars. George Bogaars would eventually become a very prominent figure in the Eurasian community back in Singapore after the war. Further up the road were more friends from home – the Rodrigues family.

In all, *Fuji-go* would be home to some 3,000 Eurasians by the time the war ended.

Although we had very few belongings, moving into our new home was both exciting and messy as there were so many little things that needed our attention. It was decided early on that Mum and us kids would be responsible for our own meals. We would of course share in the vegetables and whatever other food we could grow on our plot.

I remember Mum had her cans of corned beef and her precious leg of ham carefully tucked away. These were strictly rationed. She had also brought up quite a lot of raw white rice and together they lasted us for a surprisingly long time.

Being stuck in the middle of nowhere we had to improvise a lot. One of our first tasks was making a stove in our room. Four wooden pegs cut from an old log were used for the legs to lift it off the floor. Planks were then placed across these pegs and we moulded a thick layer of clay dug from the field to form the pit for the fire. It wasn't much to look at but our improvised stove served us well for cooking and boiling our drinking water.

While the water we drew from the stream and the well seemed clean enough, we still ran it through a home-made filter consisting of a bucket of gravel and clay before boiling it.

Alas, food still remained the biggest challenge, even though growing our own food was why we had all come all this way to Bahau. Of course no one really had any idea how to farm on this scale especially starting from scratch. There would be a lot of trial and error but we all had to start somewhere and the beginning was as good a place as any.

Sometime later Douglas would join our not-so-merry band of settlers. When he first arrived with some other single men, they were given a plot of land far off from the rest of us which was almost fringing the virgin jungle.

The men tried their best to build a simple shelter for themselves. Douglas was a scout in his younger days and as the official scout manual suggested, they tried to build a simple and quick lean-to shelter made from wooden planks leaned against each other to form an inverted V. These planks would then be lashed together with vines and rattan from the jungle for strength. It seems however that the official scout manual did not take into account the ferocity of tropical showers in this part of the world for every time it rained, which was very often, the water poured in from the open sides and all their belongings would be soaked.

The final straw came one day when a stray elephant emerged from the nearby jungle. Some settlers, especially those living on far-flung plots, had several encounters with wild elephants raiding their fields. The Long family, who were good friends of ours, had several close calls with elephants on their land. The thundering herd would cause their house to shake and when they were gone, large footprints the size of dinner plates could be seen all over their plot amidst their trampled crops.

However the elephant that Douglas encountered that day appeared to be far less threatening. It must have been nursing a serious itch and was looking for some relief. The elephant rubbed its generous bottom against his shelter which promptly fell apart.

It's funny to think about it now but back then, an elephant demolishing the home that you took days to construct was no laughing matter. This was especially so for Doug, a man who in those days didn't have much time or interest to see the lighter side of life.

Mum then had to ask Uncle Orgie for permission for Douglas to stay with us. He said it was fine as long as Douglas pulled his own weight — and that he did.

Soon another person was added to the fold. We knew of one elderly woman who had been living by herself for some time. It must have been especially tough for her to survive on her own. We felt sorry for her and invited her to stay in a small extension to the house which we built ourselves.

The crude wooden walls of our home never offered complete privacy. We kids soon found out that we could spy through the gaps in some of the walls especially those of our homemade extension. I remember once we looked into the old woman's tiny room and saw her sitting precariously in a little basin with her back to us trying to have a bath. The sight of that was so comical, it left us in stitches. I guess over there, we didn't have much to laugh about.

9

Living off the Land

Everyone, young and old, worked in the field. Our plot like all the others had been part of a steaming jungle just months earlier. The trees were cut down and the undergrowth burnt but several large stumps remained.

During the early part of the day, I helped dig the coarse soil and pull up weeds which was hot, hard work. All the women wore dresses back then even when working in the fields along with big floppy beach hats to keep the sun out of our eyes. Although these were highly impractical, they were all we had.

After a few hours and dripping with sweat, I would go back to the house to help Mum with the cooking while also looking after the young ones, Kenny and Roy. They were really wonderful children and as hard as the times were, they never complained which was a blessing.

We bought some vegetable seeds from the local shops in town and Uncle Orgie would bring up some better quality seeds whenever he came to visit. Some families would grumble about the poor soil in their fields but on our plot, the soil appeared to be quite fertile. Perhaps this area seemed to have better soil because it was closer to the stream and had a shallow underground water table or perhaps we just worked harder than some others.

Not knowing what vegetables would grow best, we planted a wide variety. These included long beans, brinjal, lady fingers, Chinese onions, sweet potatoes and tapioca. To add some flavour to our meals, we also planted chilli and pandan, both of which were very easy to grow. In our stream we found that we could cultivate *kangkong* a type of Chinese water spinach.

As part of our long term plan of self-sufficiency, we also planted a number of fruit trees. However, we did not stay in Bahau long enough to see the literal fruits of our labour.

Initially while waiting for our crops to grow, we had no choice but to buy vegetables from the Chinese who also sold chickens and even pork. We still had some money back then and whilst we suspected the pork actually came from wild boars rather than domestic pigs, food was food and no one complained. Suddenly 'floating pork' was such a treat!

One crop that we were very successful in growing was the groundnut. These hardy little bushes were easy to look after and when you pulled one up, there would be hundreds of groundnuts in their husky shells among the roots.

Most of the groundnuts were steamed and they were very sweet. I clearly remember our first groundnut harvest. Everyone was overjoyed with the results and we were all so excited with our initial success in working the land. Maybe it didn't take much to amaze us as we were such city-slickers and a long, long way from being true farmers so our initial harvest was truly momentous.

We were also all very proud of our one little claim to fame when our *bangkwang* (this is a turnip also called a yam bean in English) won first prize in one of our farming competitions. It weighed in at about 20 katis (approximately 10 kilogrammes).

The rumour at the time was that some of the boys used to urinate on the plant while it was growing and this accounted for its giant size. To this day I'm not sure if there was any truth in this story or if it was a mischievously juicy tale made up by the boys themselves just to get us all a little squeamish. I don't quite remember the taste but we must have eaten it later as we never threw food away even if it may have been tainted with a little well-meaning pee!

Tapioca and sweet potatoes were also quite easy crops to cultivate. Although rice is a staple food in this part of the world, our land was unsuitable for growing this particular crop as it needed far more water than our little stream could possibly provide. Hence we had to ration the limited amount of rice that we had brought with us and even though you could still buy rice from the shops in the village, it was costly and the quality was very poor.

To stretch our meagre supplies for as long as possible, we cooked our rice with cubes of sweet potatoes. Tapioca was another regular dish which we cut into cubes, boiled and then fried. Thin slices of our precious ham or a spoonful or two of corned beef were sometimes added as a special treat. Our meals were always very basic with little variety but they filled our stomachs nonetheless.

In later years my children would often ask why we did not hunt for food in the jungle as there were lots of monkeys around at the time. But to hunt them we would have needed a gun which we obviously didn't have. Carving out bows and arrows or building traps to catch them were far beyond our limited capabilities. We were virgin farmers barely able to eke out a living and there was no way in hell that we could outsmart a monkey, snare an angry wild boar or go head to head with an elephant. Also the dark jungle provided refuge for something far more dangerous than wild animals. It was the hunting ground of the communist guerrillas who were still opposing the Japanese occupation of Malaya. While we may not have been very savvy in attempting to live off the land, we certainly weren't suicidal enough to venture onto their turf.

Everyone had to work hard in the fields including Junior who was barely in his teens. Because of his experience in controlling mosquito breeding in Singapore, he was considered one of three essential workers in *Fuji-go* who were tasked with spraying oil in the jungle streams and marshes to kill the mosquito larvae and stem the spread of malaria. He would be out from early in the morning to noon, carrying a large tank of oil on his back and was paid a princely sum of 50 cents a day.

In the afternoon Junior would then join the other men, clearing the land, preparing the soil and tending to our meagre crops.

While we all did our best at farming each day, you could sense a change in the mood when Uncle Orgie would send word of his next visit to oversee the progress we had made. Suddenly everyone would be working a little bit harder and we womenfolk made sure the house was neat and tidy. You would get an earful from him if things were not up to the standard he expected. Still he was a good man and I don't think we could have made it had it not been for the help he gave us.

It didn't take a genius to realise that Eurasians by and large, made lousy farmers and this was painfully evident from the vegetables the community harvested. Those grown by the local Chinese farmers and sold in their shops were large, healthy and vibrant green. With a few minor exceptions like our miracle *bangkwang*, most of the vegetables grown by the Eurasian community in Bahau were sickly, pale and barely clinging to life. The indigenous Chinese farmers had been working this land for generations and I guess there were many farming secrets that we simply did not know and probably never would.

Sonya aged two with her father Arthur Henry Nunes

Staging concerts and plays at home for friends and neighbours were part of growing up before the war. This was Halloween in 1932 in Saint Barnabas Road. (From left): Henry, Sonya (dressed as Miss Good Luck), Maisie, Margie and Junior

Douglas Miller was a scout and avid sportsman in his younger days

The Convent of the Holy Infant Jesus where many Eurasian women and children sought refuge was bombed several times in the early weeks of the war

Many homes were destroyed during the Japanese bombing campaign of Singapore

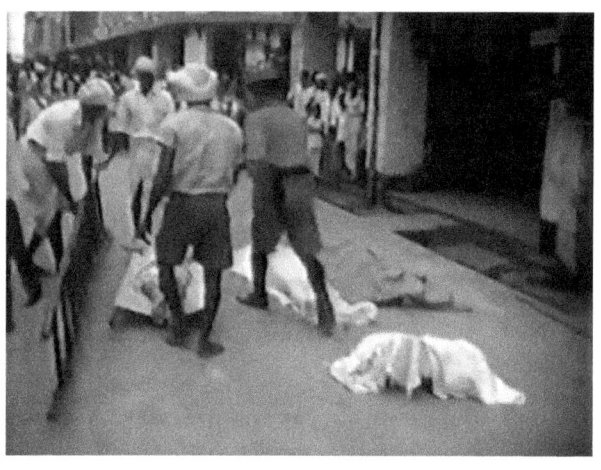

Hundreds of civilians attempted to flee the island by ship in the weeks before the surrender in February 1942

British Lieutenant-General Arthur Percival (back to camera) meeting Lieutenant-General Yamashita minutes before the unconditional surrender of Singapore in 1942

Japanese Type 95 Ha-Go tanks parading through Singapore soon after the surrender on February 15 1942

The total number of civilians killed or injured in the Japanese invasion of Singapore will never be known

Thousands of Allied solders were marched through the streets towards Changi Prison after the surrender of Singapore

Some Allied POWs were put to work clearing the rubble from many destroyed buildings

In 1962 the remains of many civilians killed during the Japanese Occupation were unearthed. The Civilian War Memorial (above) was erected in their honour. It was unveiled on February 15 1967 – the 25th anniversary of the Fall of Singapore

Typical propaganda reports in the Japanese-run newspapers shortly after the Occupation began

M.A.D. (Syonan-to) NOTICE No. 12

REWARD

Anyone who knows anything about a Nipponese aeroplane lost between Dec 23 1941 and Jan 10 1942 in the jungle in the vicinity of Johore Bahru and Syonan-to is requested to report particulars to the Head Officer of the Nippon Military Administration Department, Municipal Office Syonan-to. Anyone who furnishes particulars which may lead to the discovery of the lost plane shall be rewarded.

BY ORDER

A sample of the MAD notices run daily by the Military Administration Department in Occupied Singapore

With Singapore facing a critical shortage of food, even the Padang was turned into a communal farm

Some members of the dreaded Kempeitai in Singapore

New arrivals in Bahau were housed in communal longhouses like these while waiting to be allocated a plot of land

Eurasian women working in the fields in Bahau

Sonya and Douglas were married on November 16 1946 about a year after returning from Bahau

The photograph above was taken in the late 1950's: (Standing from left) Sonya, Junior and Mabel. (Seated from left) Roy, Noreen and Kenny

Taken in 2009: (Standing from left: Kenny, Junior and Roy (Seated from left) Noreen and Sonya

(Above left) Mabel Nunes and Bishop Devals (right)

Some members of the clan at a gathering in Bukit Timah in 1964

A replica of one of the 15-inch coastal guns that the British destroyed shortly before their surrender to prevent these weapons from falling into Japanese hands

A Page One report on the discovery of a war bunker in 1992
– Reporting by David Miller

10

The Bahau Beat

Life in Bahau moved to its own beat, one that was often slow and mind-numbingly monotonous.

Our life was guided by routines. Waking up in the morning, we had to draw water for boiling and make the fire. Every morning I would see Douglas going out to cut some firewood for us and then he would grumble about the bluntness of the old axe. Most of the time the wood was still green and getting it to burn took some effort, skill and very often, sheer luck.

The Perry's used to wake up very early to make their cooking fire and sometimes when no one was looking, we would send Junior over to steal some of it. He would take a few of their burning sticks, put it in his little metal bucket and run back to our room to feed our little improvised stove. It saved us a lot of time and soon Junior became quite an expert at acquiring fire. As far as I know, I don't think he was ever caught!

Mum tried rearing our own chickens so that we could add a little fresh meat to our diet. Whilst she had no qualms about it, I don't think she enjoyed killing the chickens but simply saw it as something that needed to be done. Alas we kids used to cry so much when she would take a knife to one of our beloved chickens that we ended up keeping the remaining ones as pets and they rewarded us with eggs in return.

The Good Shepherd nuns who ran the little convent in the village also operated a tiny school where Kenny studied and became a good student. There was a gong outside the school that someone had to strike every hour on the hour during the day and this in a sense became the equivalent of the village clock.

Later on Roy would be enrolled in its pre-school class of sorts but he proved to be a handful. He didn't spend much time in school as he was always crying and wanting to come back home. Inevitably someone would come running to our house and tell us to take him back as he was causing too much of a distraction for the other children. The next day of course, he would pretend to have some illness to avoid being sent back to the school.

There were some brothers from Saint Patrick's School in Singapore staying in the settlement along with a few priests. I dreaded each time a priest would come over to visit our home because he would always ask us young ones why we weren't attending their catechism classes.

Douglas was close friends with the priests and brothers. More importantly, he was on good terms with the man who helped out with the cooking for them. On his way home every evening, this man would stop by our house and give us some leftover bread or buns or any food that was uneaten.

I remember sometimes Auntie Josephine would announce that she wanted to go into the town. Now she was a very large woman and there was no way that she could walk the eight hilly kilometres to Bahau on her own, so we would borrow someone's cart and all of us young ones would push her along the road. It was fun and a good break from the daily farming routine.

In the evenings when all the work was done for the day, we would gather on the veranda of our house and look out across the field and the jungle beyond. There was a long wooden bench with the bark still attached that we used to sit on.

We were in the midst of nature – raw, beautiful and untamed. We could hear the monkeys who kept up a constant chatter and sometimes we would see them in the distance, jumping from tree to tree.

Then of course there were the occasional raids by elephants. One of their favourite foods was the sugar cane which many families planted in clumps. People would have to go out and knock on saucepans in an attempt to drive these stubborn animals back to the jungle. Luckily our plot was never raided and I personally never saw an elephant all the time I was in Bahau.

I did hear of one story concerning a confrontation with a tiger. Apparently some people came face to face with a tiger which wandered onto their plot of land and whilst it must have caused a stir, the animal simply turned and walked away back to its jungle home. Perhaps the tiger realised that its intended victims were just skin and bones and hardly worth the trouble.

As we all gathered on the veranda for our evening break, Douglas and some of the other men would be playing poker. Everyone else would be talking about Singapore and our life there before this horrible war changed everything. Even the younger ones like Kenny and Noreen would chip in reminiscing about the 'good ole days' and all the fun we used to have.

Mum of course would throw a damp towel on the conversation by reminding them in no uncertain terms: "Yes and if you all were still in Singapore, you would be studying now instead of doing nothing!" Truth be told, we did bring our school books with us but in reality not much studying was ever done.

I remember the nights were always cool in Bahau. As the sun went down and the mosquitoes came out, we would burn some of the undergrowth that we cleared from the fields. The smoke from the fire would help a little in keeping the mosquitoes at bay. By this time, the younger ones would have gone off to sleep and the conversation would drift along with someone always asking if we could remember this incident or that person. We would all talk about our life now, how different it all was and what other surprises fate still held in store for us. The smiles of the evening would inevitably fade and soon everyone would be left feeling frustrated and depressed.

We were so cut off from civilisation and news of the outside world. Uncle Orgie would tell us about the little that he had heard from Singapore but even that was very scant. Out here in the middle of nowhere, seemingly abandoned and forgotten – this life in limbo was the only reality we knew and there was no end in sight.

It bothered me that we all seemed to be losing hope. I remember sometimes, as young as I was, I would try to lighten the mood. "All of you sitting here today and grumbling – just remember, soon all of us will be going back home. Then we will say that Bahau was just a dream – we never could have done all that." Yes, I was quite a firecracker back then but the others would just scoff at me saying I was too young to understand what was really going on.

"Nah, you don't know what you are talking about!" Reggie would reply. He was always putting me down like that but I would stand my ground saying: "You wait and see. We will make it and then we will be able to tell our children what we did in Bahau."

Still no one believed me – believed that we would make it out of this place alive. In my heart, I didn't either.

Eventually the fireflies would come out, so would the guitars and we would sing into the night. It was the only source of entertainment we had and this was the time of the day that I always looked forward to, because it seemed … well … normal.

Douglas too used to sing. He couldn't carry a tune to save his life and he would make up his own lyrics some of which made no sense at all. But no one would bat an eyelid as it was all in good fun and kept our spirits high enough to plod on for yet another day. Such was the dreary life in Bahau.

11

Singing in the Loo

Many years after Bahau was to become just a distant fading memory, I would tell my children about the tough times we had there. It is hard to imagine life without a tap with clean drinking water, electricity available at the flick of a switch or a flushing toilet. We had none of those things in Bahau.

Back then, going to the toilet was a chore you tended to put off for as long as possible because it was so unpleasant. But one can only ignore the call of nature for so long before those shouts become deafening.

The toilet was an outhouse where you ventured in at your own peril. It was more like a tiny shed, a cubicle with a large hole dug in the ground. One false step and the whole adventure would take a nasty turn for the worse.

For reasons that are still beyond me, the toilet door never had a lock. To prevent embarrassing encounters with another family member, you had to sing or whistle loudly so everyone else would know that it was occupied. Yes, really.

My children in later years would always ask what we used for toilet paper and in all honesty, I can't remember. Perhaps that would account for the disappearing schoolbooks!

One thing I can never forget was the overpowering smell of the toilet. It would get into your clothes and in your hair – a horrible, suffocating stench of raw human waste that never seemed to go away.

The only thing worse than going to the outhouse, was going to the outhouse at night. There was no electricity and candles were rare and expensive so we used palm oil instead. We would pour just a little of the blood red oil in a saucer, add a wick which was just a little piece of leftover rope and when the oil soaked through, you could light it. It provided very little illumination but it was still the best alternative we had. You would then carry this contraption to the toilet and pray to all the saints watching above that the little flickering light would not go out before the deed was done. Yes we sure prayed a lot in those days for a great many little things.

The toilet did serve one other important function. With no fertiliser to be had, we had to rely on more 'organic' alternatives. Thankfully this job was left to the men to handle.

Smell aside, our humble toilet was a marvel of primitive engineering. From the main hole which you squatted over, the men fashioned pipes made from the bark of trees held together with rattan so that the 'contents' would flow into another open holding tank dug in the ground a few metres away. From there, once a certain limit was reached, it would flow into a third tank. By this time, the waste would have been diluted with rain water and when that was full, it could be scooped up and spread in the field.

The smell of those times would stay in my memory forever. Even days later, the odour from the field would be just as strong as ever and you tried your best not to think of that smell or its origins when you were eating the vegetables grown in that same patch of soiled earth. Such was life.

Curiously, Douglas would always be sick on those days when the little outhouse was due to be cleared out.

12

Weddings and Funerals

In fleeing to Bahau, most of us figured that we could escape the wrath of the Japanese and the abject cruelty and torture of the dreaded *Kempeitai*. In a way we were right. There were hardly any Japanese soldiers around and the few that we saw in and around the settlement never bothered us. I guess they were content to leave us alone as long as we did not cause any trouble for them.

These soldiers had a small hall to themselves and sometimes they would invite people over. They even had a record player for listening to music from home. "Teach us sing English songs," they would say to us in their broken English.

Now I know that some people have written about their experiences in Bahau decades later and would describe our little *Fuji-go* settlement as a harsh internment centre, a concentration camp of sorts but this was not my experience, nor my recollection. For the most part, the Japanese guards left us alone. Unlike the troops stationed in Singapore, these guys were obviously not crack frontline fighters but more likely second-stringers tasked with handling the routine jobs like looking after a bunch of harmless civilians who were still trying to figure out how to be farmers.

Some guards tried to make friends by offering drinks and cigarettes to the adults and goodies like chocolates and biscuits from their rations to the children. These soldiers would show us their well-worn photographs of their families and the children who were waiting for them back home. They would gather in groups smoking contently during our little concerts, nodding along to the unfamiliar music. They had wanted to learn our language and some could speak passable English by the time the war ended. I don't think this was a ploy to win over our hearts and minds; they were probably just as tired of this sorry war and as homesick as we all were.

But in coming to Bahau we had in essence exchanged the fear of dying at the hands of the brutal Japanese in Singapore with the very real prospect of dying from malaria and malnutrition out here in the jungle.

Right from the very start, when we were still living in the longhouses waiting for our homes to be built, people started coming down with malaria. It began slowly, just one or two at a time but soon as we all got weaker from the exhausting work and poor nutrition, the mosquitoes began taking their toll.

With malaria spread by the bite of the Aedes mosquito, a person begins to feel extremely weak. There would be fits of shivering alternating with bouts of intense sweating and high fever. Quinine was the medication of choice administered usually as pills. Sometimes you could get it in liquid form which tasted horrible but was apparently more potent.

This jungle illness would leave you bedridden for a few days and even after recovery, you were more than likely to continue to feel lethargic for at least a few more days. With prompt treatment, most fit people could expect to pull through.

But malaria can easily prove fatal when the victim was weak, undernourished or overworked to begin with and that was exactly what we all were in Bahau. Even the children like Kenny and Roy were reduced to just skin and bones after only a few months in the jungle.

It seemed that almost everyone came down with malaria. Junior was the only person I can remember who never had it. The moment it began to get dark and the mosquitoes started buzzing, Junior would retreat to his tiny room and stay under his mosquito net which is probably why he never caught this deadly bug.

Said Junior: "Yes, I got teased a lot by the Perry boys for heading to bed at 5.30 in the evening and staying under my mosquito net, but I always remembered what an aunt told me after my father passed away. She said I was now the head of the family and I knew I had to stay healthy to look after the others. The boys may have laughed at me but I was the one that helped to carry them to the clinic when they got sick.

"I remember once one of them came down with Blackwater Fever, a more serious form of malaria. He was delirious and we covered him with a blanket to keep him warm on the stretcher. Carrying him feet first into the clinic, one of the two nurses there stopped us saying 'No, No. Dead bodies go to the mortuary.' Our little patient must have heard this for he sat up immediately declaring: 'But I'm not dead!' It was such a sight!"

There was very little medicine but whatever was available, was given out free of charge by the nurses to those who needed it. I think some people were just waiting to get sick just so they could get a few days of rest. It was better for our family because we were a rather large group so when someone fell ill, there were always others who could step up and get the work done.

This was not the case for many others – especially those families consisting of just a husband and wife like that old couple Diddle and the Fiddle. Eventually some small families simply had to give up. Some abandoned their land to stay in the village and were looked after by the brothers and the nuns.

So many people there died of malaria or other tropical diseases. The mosquitoes could breed in just a coin-sized puddle of stagnant water and there were huge swaths of wet jungle surrounding us for them to do just that. Others fell ill from various parasites when they drank water that was not properly filtered and boiled.

One estimate which we learnt later revealed that of the 3,000 people who were in Bahau, between 300 and 500 never made it home. This works out to be about one death every two days. The exact number of fatalities would probably never be known.

One of the most prominent members of the Bahau settlement to perish was Bishop Adrian Devals. He suffered a farming injury to his foot which became infected and without a proper hospital in Bahau he died of tetanus in January 1945.

With our family plot located so close to the village, Douglas and my cousin Charlie would often be summoned by the priests. It was always the same reason – someone had died and they were asked to carry the body to the church. It was usually a long walk from the person's home to the church with many hills in between but the men never complained about this additional work. Death was just another stark reality of our time in Bahau.

Once Douglas was told that one of his good friends, a Dane by the name of Kobish, had passed away. He had been staying with the brothers in the centre of the settlement as he had a very hard time adjusting to the spartan life in Bahau. He was a big man with a large frame when he arrived but he had been reduced to a walking skeleton just before his death.

When Douglas reached the church, he saw that his friend's body had been laid out naked on a table. He asked one of the priests what had happened to the man's clothes. The priest said that after the man passed away, they dressed him up but then someone apparently came by later and stole all his clothes.

On hearing this, Douglas was very distraught. He immediately went back home, took one of the few precious long sleeved shirts and a pair of trousers that he had left and gave it to the priest. "Let him be buried with some dignity," he said. I still get choked up when I think of this incident. Douglas, for all his temper and fussy ways, was a very good and kind man at heart.

There was a group of young boys staying in *Fuji-go* who were looked after by the brothers at a hut we called Boys' Town. They were either orphaned or had been sent there for their own safety while their families remained in Singapore. One of their jobs was to dig graves which earned them a few cents. But these boys were all very weak. So when it came to digging a grave for Kobish, it was dug with tapering sides and when his large coffin was lowered, it became firmly wedged in about a metre from the bottom of the hole.

"Someone had to go in and widen the grave and being young and fit, I was asked to do it," said Junior. "I had to crawl under the coffin and using just a small spade, I dug into the sides of the grave widening the walls slowly while praying that the wooden box would not fall on my head."

I remember when we passed by the small cemetery, we would all instinctively avert our gaze as no one wanted to think about death any more than we had to. It was all around us and sadly, very much a part of our lives.

Sometimes the ever-present spectre of death would play tricks on people. We had an elderly aunt called Verolinda or Auntie Inda for short. I think she almost died three times in Bahau. We would suddenly be called out: "Children come quickly. Your Aunt Inda is dying!"

So Junior, Kenny, Noreen, Gwen, Roy and I would rush to her home and there she would be lying on her bed looking as pale as death itself and apparently gasping for her last breath. Another aunt would tell us all to line up near the bed and pray so we would all clasp our hands together. With our eyes turned up to the heavens above we would pray fervently: "Jesus, Mary and Joseph. Come and save our aunt!" We would then be told to cry so we would rub our eyes trying to force some tears out. Our tears and prayers must have worked for in just a few minutes, the 'dying' aunt would be up and about and things would return to normal.

I don't know if this was one of those wartime miracles you hear about but I'm guessing it probably wasn't. It was probably just depression. Anyway, after her speedy recovery, we were then free to go so we would head out and play in her garden for a while before returning home to the usual routine of life.

There were also more than a few weddings in Bahau. One of the first couples to get married was Luke de Souza and Florence Chopard. He had to walk some miles in his suit to get to the church and she wore a long gown that the nuns helped to sew. After the wedding ceremony at the church, there was a big celebration but us younger ones could only watch the festivities from a distance because we weren't invited. Sigh.

13

Making Money

Apparently one of the reasons Bahau was chosen for the resettlement camp was because the Japanese were building an airfield nearby at a place called Josei. The grand plan, or at least the rumour we heard was that the Japanese had planned to fly all the excess produce from Bahau to meet the rising demand for food in Singapore. This seemed highly unlikely and was probably just that, a rumour. In the miraculous event that *Fuji-*

go could actually produce any excess food, it would have been more economical to transport it by train.

But the fact remained that the Japanese were building an airfield not far from our resettlement camp and 'volunteers' would regularly be scheduled to go and work there for a day. The Japanese really didn't care who actually went and who didn't as long as there were sufficient men present for the day, so those who had money when it was their turn to go would pay someone else to take their place. Douglas, who was 22 at the time, went off frequently for such day jobs. It was tough work but he was glad to get some hard cash in hand by replacing some lazy fellow.

I remember I would always stand at the balcony and cry as he went carrying his little kettle and his lunch and wearing a frown. It was not dangerous but any work done under the supervision of the unfamiliar Japanese soldiers who were guarding the airfield, carried some risks.

I was so glad to see him return at the end of the day and although he would always be grumbling about the work they had to do, it was good to have him home. As far as I know, that airfield was never completed.

Many Eurasians sold whatever they could to the locals in Bahau and Kuala Pilah just to get some extra cash and we were no exception. My haul of toothbrushes and soap came in handy making us a few dollars when money was tight. Mum sold some spare bed sheets, pillowcases and curtains to help make ends meet. Some of the clothes we had brought up from Singapore like lace dresses were very precious to us but they were totally impractical for life here so eventually those too were sold. Douglas never had much in the way of possessions but he too was forced to sell off his few belongings including one prized bicycle.

Junior had a more enterprising way of making some cash. He would go house to house in *Fuji-go* asking people if they had anything to sell. He would then take these to the town and sell it to the locals making a few dollars in commission for his efforts.

Once Mum borrowed Douglas's scout hat because she was going into the village and it was another hot day. There she met a man who took a fancy to the hat and offered to buy it. Mum thought it was a great deal and promptly sold it.

She came back home excitedly telling us about it when Douglas hit the roof. I had never seen him so angry before. I guess when you have so little in life your few possessions become even more precious. It took Douglas a long time to calm down about losing his cherished hat which was now sitting on someone else's head and even years later, when the subject of his missing hat came up, you could tell that it still bothered him.

Some people did try to make money in other ways. One of our neighbours had the bright idea of opening a tea garden in front of his house for people to buy a cup and chat.

They asked Mum if she was willing to make some snacks to be sold there. We gave it a try selling *popiah* (a type of spring roll), fried bananas and some cakes. My younger sister Noreen, who was 13 at the time, was put in charge of manning the cake stand – a decision that did not go down well with her.

"Why can't Sonya go? Just because she has a boyfriend, so I have to go?" she objected loudly. And even now, more than 70 years later, when that subject comes up in conversation, she would still be grumbling about how at that tender age, she had been put to work.

Apart from selling the cakes in the tea garden Noreen also had to go house to house hawking whatever was left over which was not as difficult a job as it sounds. Inevitably one of the richer Eurasian families would feel a little sorry for her and buy the lot. She would then return home triumphant in having made a little money for the family.

Sadly the tea garden closed after just a month because most of the Eurasians our neighbours were depending on as their customers, simply did not have the spare cash to splurge on a cup of tea.

Of course there were others who were more successful in setting up a business. There was the Rodrigues family who ran a sundry shop and they did very well. They sold onions and potatoes along with lots of other stuff. Gwen, my cousin, was hired to man the counter but I think she took home more of the merchandise than she actually sold.

I remember she was always rolling *Assam* balls – a type of sourish sweet made from fruit that was frequently used in cooking at the time. Moe (Maurice), another cousin, would always be at the shop on the pretence of helping Gwen out but truth be told, he would be helping himself to the 'free' *kanak* (dried fruits) and *Assam* balls.

Being as young as we were, we weren't too bothered about money. If we had some it was great; if we didn't, which was usually the case, we just learnt to do without.

However our financial situation or lack of one, affected the adults differently. Mum for instance always seemed bothered when we would look longingly at some of the other children in *Fuji-go* with their nice clothes and new toys brought up from Singapore while we were always looking somewhat scruffy and a little worse for wear.

Still we counted ourselves to be more fortunate than some of the others. We survived there because we had the manpower – strong young men willing to go out in the sun-baked field and do the tough work without complaining. The older families especially those on their own like Diddle and the Fiddle, had a really tough time. Whatever they planted, it all died and their houses would be falling apart. Many would simply lose hope. Maybe it was this total surrender to the situation and the utter despair that killed more people than malaria ever did. I don't know. Sigh.

I am doubtful that we too would have made it had this terrible war continued for another year or two. After surviving in Bahau for just a few months, we were already almost out of things to sell. Our threadbare clothes were starting to fall off our backs in this hot and humid climate. Even if you wanted to mend your clothes, you still needed needles and thread which like everything else, was either expensive or in short supply or both. The long trousers that the men wore became shorter and shorter as sections were cut off from the bottom to mend holes higher up.

Eventually the Bahau community turned to the Japanese and pleaded for some cloth so we could make our own clothes. Surprisingly they agreed but the cloth they eventually gave us turned out to be more like a very stiff type of canvas. They said it was 'very good, very good' but you could barely get a needle through it.

Still beggars could not be choosers so instead of the usual long trousers, a new fashion trend soon emerged among the men by sheer necessity rather than choice. The cloth was turned into *sarongs* – essentially long, wraparound skirts similar to those worn by the indigenous Malay community. It was quite amusing seeing so many men all walking around in the same navy blue *sarongs*. Whilst there is a certain technique for tying these *sarongs* so they won't slip off, ours were just held up with big safety pins used for diapers and modesty for the most part, was preserved.

14

Sweet Content

While things in *Fuji-go* were really difficult, we all tried to make the best of the situation. There were often concerts for the people to lift our spirits and foster better communal ties. The Japanese soldiers would also attend, sitting quietly by themselves and listening to the music.

At one concert, I sang the song *Timber* by Ferlin Husky with some boys providing the music on their guitars. Not long after the concert was over and I was walking with Douglas to the shops, some boys would tease me calling out "Timmmberrr!"

Douglas, being a very protective person, would of course get angry with these mischievous boys but nothing bad happened. As far as I can recall, there were hardly any fights or major crimes in the settlement apart from some petty thefts.

Being stuck in the middle of the jungle, there were no addresses to our houses. Someone came up with the idea that we should each give a name to our respective homes. They even had a competition just to get everyone to participate.

I decided to call ours 'Sweet Content' because, at least in my opinion, we were so content there and everyone was so sweet. I even came up with a poem to go with the name. It went like this:

When you are old and in two you are bent
Think of the days you spent in Sweet Content.
When malaria was at its highest and lo!
Made you regret ever going to Fuji-go.

I wrote out the poem on a piece of paper and pasted it outside our home and it won the first prize. I have never forgotten that poem and it still brings back memories of our little jungle home.

Soon all the houses had names and it was beginning to feel more like a real village of sorts. Further down the road lived a group of young men. They had all come up together but they never seemed to do any work at all. I'm not sure how they survived and were able to feed themselves being as lazy as they were. They called their home "The Slackers' Retreat" which I suppose was quite appropriate.

We had been living in Bahau now for almost ten months and soon it was time for Christmas. We didn't have much of a Christmas tree as far as I can remember. Maybe it was just a branch that we decorated as best we could.

Everyone was dressed in their best clothes for the Midnight Mass as it was such a special event. Even the youngsters from Boys' Town were there standing at the back of the church and feeling a little out of place. They were wearing the best shirts they had but in reality, these seemed to be more like rags. It was sad looking or rather trying not to look at them and it made us count our blessings, few though these were.

There was a lot of singing during the service and it was a very simple Christmas celebration – perhaps the way it was always meant to be. In that small wooden church, in the middle of that steaming hot jungle amidst the faint glow of candles that kept the darkness at bay, we gathered hand in hand singing the hauntingly beautiful refrains *Gloria in Excelsis Deo* in perfect harmony. In a strange way, it was the most beautiful Christmas celebration ever and everyone must have shed more than a few silent tears of thanks to the unseen angels who had kept watch over us all these long and painful months. We were still alive and as hard as life was in Bahau, for that one magical night, just being alive seemed to be enough to remind us that we weren't alone.

There were hardly any new toys for the younger ones but still, it was our first and thankfully only Christmas that we spent in the jungle.

A few days later and we were celebrating again at the New Year's Eve party to welcome

1945 with glasses of *samsu*, an illicit alcoholic concoction. Towards the end of the celebration, all the adults gathered began singing *'There'll always be an England'*. This was a patriotic song written in the summer of 1939 and it became very popular upon the outbreak of World War II.

Sure there was some lingering resentment that the British were not able to defend Singapore as they had promised and we were left in this predicament, but the song gave us reason to hope that our long wait to return to a normal life back home would not be in vain.

It was soon the middle of 1945 and cut off as we were from the outside world we didn't know that the Pacific War was already winding down.

Douglas had proposed and I of course accepted. We were engaged in August that year just before the war officially ended. It was another excuse to celebrate and wow, did the boys go all out decorating the house! I even had to stay somewhere else for a day so they could finish the job and surprise me.

Traditional wedding decorations were of course in short supply but we did have fruits and flowers and they made great use of these to trim the entire house. It was beautiful and I was very touched by all the hard work everyone had put in.

The priest came over and blessed us but the actual engagement ceremony had to be postponed because the fellow that Douglas had asked to bring the ring from Singapore, had come up for the party but had forgotten all about the ring! So we had to wait for someone else who would be travelling to Bahau to bring the ring before we were officially engaged.

Still the celebration went off well with lots of food. Our beloved ham which was still going strong also made an appearance. It was surprising that the ham lasted so many months and never went mouldy in the damp conditions we were living in. I remember Mum would take the ham out every day just so it could get a little sun and stay dry. Yes, we were all very protective over our little ham.

15

The Wings of Peace

Junior was in the town one day trying to sell some old clothes to a shopkeeper who was one of his regular buyers.

"But the man waved his hands and told me '*tak mau, tak mau*'. This is Malay for 'don't want'. So I asked him why and he said '*Habis – sudah habis*' meaning 'It's over'. He then told me that Japan had surrendered and the British were coming back. I jumped on my bicycle and sped back to *Fuji-go* to spread the word," recalled Junior.

At first people in the settlement were sceptical but soon we saw the Malay policeman in *Fuji-go* who worked for the Japanese, hastily packing his things and leaving without a word. It was the communists who came by a little later that night and confirmed the surrender. Still we had very few details as to what had actually happened. No one told us about the two atomic bombs that were dropped on Hiroshima and Nagasaki – we only learnt of these much later.

To say we were all overjoyed by the news that this long and terrible war was now over, would be an understatement. Against all the odds and the Japanese and the Malayan jungle and the parasites and the mosquitoes, we had made it – just barely.

While everyone was happy, there was still much uncertainty about our fate and what the Japanese may do to us before they left.

Thankfully that question was put to rest a few days later when the Japanese called a meeting for the whole settlement. I don't think they actually used the word 'surrender' but instead they said they were soon to leave the country and they hope God would look kindly on them and within hours, they were gone.

They did not ask for forgiveness for the atrocities committed during their invasion and occupation of Singapore. I had the feeling that some of these guards did feel some remorse for all that had happened. Would we have forgiven them had we been asked? Probably not – at least not then. That wound would take many years to heal.

The Japanese had told us not to panic and that arrangements would soon be made to send us back to Singapore. We were all ecstatic that finally after about one and a half years in this desolate place, we were really going home.

As soon as the Japanese left, the nuns who had been hiding a large Union Jack all these months quickly hoisted the flag and we all stood around cheering.

To celebrate, a Gala Victory Dance was quickly organised. Everyone attended sharing food and dancing to the music provided by our very own Bahau band.

Even before we left Singapore for Bahau, we were told at one of the many briefings that guerrillas from the Malayan People's Anti-Japanese Army (MPAJA) were operating in that part of the jungle and they would be close to our settlement.

In no uncertain terms we were all warned to steer clear of them, to remain neutral and avoid talking about politics or the war to any outsiders. To be seen siding with the Japanese or the communists or worse still, the British, could very easily get you killed.

From time to time we did see some of these men around our settlement whom we were told were communists. They never wore uniforms or carried guns. On the whole, they seemed decent enough and they did not bother us at all. In fact, they were very kind to the children, sometimes giving them chocolates. The communists were also fond of music and they would bring their guitars and play alongside the Eurasian musicians.

While the communists seemed to be friendly, one incident reminded us all that things and people were not always as they appear to be. This happened soon after the Japanese had left.

Apparently somebody had spread a rumour that certain individuals in *Fuji-go* were listening to the radio and for some reason this was a big issue for the communists.

They called an immediate meeting in which everyone had to attend. Some of their officers acted as judges in what took on the appearance of an impromptu trial in which they singled out three people from our settlement as suspects. One was an old woman and another was a good friend of ours Willy Ess, who would later become the best man at our wedding. I can't recall who the third person was.

We were all asked to say if they were guilty or not. If we said they were guilty, they would certainly be taken into the jungle and be killed. I remember many of us cried and begged them to let these three go as they were all innocent. Eventually the communists relented and warned us all not to listen to the radio.

Looking back, I don't think the communist knew who, if anyone had been listening to the radio. They just wanted to make an example to scare us and it worked.

With the war now ended and the British due to return any day, the communists too must have been worried about their uncertain future. Many would retreat back into their jungle sanctuary ready to continue their fight against a new adversary – the British.

We soon received word that the British army would be arriving. We were told to mark a large white T in an open space close to the centre of the settlement.

A few hours later six fully-armed paratroopers landed. The first thing they did after they hit the ground was to point their guns at us. We must have looked like animals to them being so thin and smelly with our clothes falling off our backs! But these six men were army medics and they soon got down to treating the sick, the weak and the starving.

These soldiers gave us lots of chocolates. A little later we had some military rations distributed to us. I remember we were all so amazed to get these ready-packed meals. You lifted up the cover, lit a small wick and you had a warm meal in minutes.

And then things only got better.

We could hear them in the distance, Allied planes flying low heading towards us from the jungle horizon. Then tiny parachutes would appear out the back. We would all be screaming and waving, waiting excitedly as the parachutes grew larger.

The chutes attached to large metal cylinders would drift down gently, landing in many of the fields. Everyone would be out rushing towards them. It really felt like a belated Christmas with presents aplenty falling from the sky.

These supply drops contained much food, blankets, medicine and clothes, more than enough to go around. We hadn't eaten well for so many months and now suddenly there was so much available. Some people stuffed themselves till they got sick and then they came back and ate some more.

Everyone would be scrambling to see what was in the next hamper still floating towards us. After one such parachute drop, Roy came back home proudly showing us a pair of used leather loafers he had found, the kind that grandfathers would probably wear. Still several sizes too big, he was so happy walking around in his new pair of shoes – his first in years.

After months of scrounging to make a living, it was a time of plenty and these were some of the best memories of the war.

I don't know how they managed it but within days of being told of the Japanese surrender, the Chinese settlers among us had suddenly disappeared without a word. They had all gone back to Singapore.

It was now time for us to make plans to do the same. Our lives which had been put on hold for so many months would soon be restarted. We had some really smart fellows among us who stepped up to take charge and they were the ones who began making all the necessary arrangements for an orderly return home.

The repatriation of the Eurasian community from Bahau took much longer than expected and it wasn't until October that we were finally told to pack up all our things.

While we never thought we had a lot of stuff in Bahau, packing up told a completely different story. As they wanted to fit as many people as possible in the train carriages, each person was only allowed to carry a small bag on board. We were told that the rest of our belongings should be left at a certain place near the railway station and these would be taken as cargo back to Singapore on the same train. We packed up as many bags and boxes as we could.

Sadly not one box or a single bag ever made it back to Singapore. Even our precious ham had gone missing. We never had a chance to say our goodbyes and our thanks for keeping us fed through some of the darkest days of our lives.

Like many of the other returning Eurasians, we had lost practically everything. Rumour had it that the villagers at Bahau must have stolen most of our luggage before it could be loaded onto the train. We just had the clothes on our backs and the little suitcases that we carried. Douglas too had lost everything. He only had a now worthless Japanese $5 note in his pocket when he set foot again in Singapore.

16

Coming Home

Like many other returning refugees, we waited for hours at the train station to see if our missing luggage could be found. Eventually we had to accept the bitter truth. We were about to resume our lives and yet again, we would be starting from scratch.

Douglas went home to live with his family in Mackenzie Road. Uncle Orgie came to pick us up and we were offered temporary accommodation at a friend's home in Kampong Java Road. We went there for dinner and stayed for a few days.

The small Eurasian community in Singapore was whole once again although our numbers had been decimated by the war. Still the Eurasian Association went to great lengths to keep the communal ties strong.

The Eurasian Youth Movement organised a number of sporting competitions and singing contests. We were grouped according to where we stayed and the performances were held at Victoria School. The Katong group was always the strongest having the best athletes, singers and dancers. There were other groups like those representing Bukit Timah. We were in Serangoon group which was seriously lacking in talent!

Things were still very tough for our family and Mum had to register for financial aid.

Eventually she took a job for a short while working as a waitress at the John Little Department Store. At that time the store also operated a restaurant complete with a dance floor patronised mainly by the British troops. Some time later she and Noreen went to work at Universal Cars in Orchard Road where the Dhoby Ghaut MRT Station now stands.

Soon after we got back from Bahau, I wanted to return to school but Douglas was dead set against that idea as he wanted us to get married as soon as possible. By this time, Mum and the rest of us had moved back in with the Perry's in their Thomson Road home.

It was about a year after we returned from Bahau that Douglas and I were married at Saint Joseph's Cathedral on November 16 1946. He started working in the civil service and he would keep that same job till he retired at the age of 72.

After the wedding I moved in to stay with Douglas's family, the Millers, in McKenzie Road. In the six years that we stayed there, I had three children – Valerie, Brian and Merlyn. We then moved to Upper Serangoon Road where we lived in half a garage and there my fourth child Priscilla was born.

We finally had a house to call our own in 1954 when we were given government quarters in Towner Road. Soon the family grew even larger with the births of Christopher, Gary, Luanna and David. Together with Mum, we moved again settling into a large bungalow with many fruit trees in Bukit Timah in 1962 where my last child Sharon was born a year later. We would stay there for more than 30 contented years.

My brother Junior did return to school and eventually became a teacher and a principal. Both Kenny and Roy would leave Singapore for London in the 1960s. Kenny eventually settled in the United States while Junior, Noreen and Roy migrated to Australia and are all happily married.

At the age of 87, Mum passed away on May 31 1992 leaving behind her legacy of five children, 22 grandchildren, 28 great-grandchildren and a great-great granddaughter.

Douglas would pass away in his sleep on May 4 2009, also at the age of 87. Both of us were in Perth, Australia celebrating Junior's 80th birthday.

Looking back, the time we spent in Bahau does seem like a dream now – a foggy and surreal episode, one that had been buried and largely forgotten for decades.

In retelling this story I have tried my best to recall both the good times and the bad for which there were many. I have tried as accurately as my memory permits to record for my family all the little details of my experiences during that war – the happy and the sad times along with the funny and the smelly episodes.

I always knew in my heart that one day I would tell my children, my children's children and hopefully they would in turn tell generations thereafter of that unforgettable time of Bahau, the elephant and the ham.

X X X

17

In Retrospect

The story of Bahau would be incomplete without understanding why so many Eurasians who were totally clueless about working the land, opted to head north and start a totally different life in a rural farming community deep in the hostile Malayan jungle.

There were both push and pull factors carefully orchestrated by the Japanese propaganda machine targeted specifically at the Eurasian and Chinese communities.

In the early stages of the Japanese Occupation the main English daily newspaper, *The Syonan Times* later renamed *The Syonan Shimbun,* frequently ran stories against these communities with thinly-veiled threats of further punishment.

This stance softened later in September 1943 when the Endau and subsequently the Bahau initiatives were proposed. The newspaper would go on to publish many stories, much of it pure propaganda, encouraging Eurasians to volunteer for Bahau promising that it would be a positive start in a land of 'paradise'. Often it would quote unnamed Eurasians on how happy they were with their idyllic life in Bahau and the 'romance of this rural scenery'.

Given the harsh conditions of life in Singapore with its critical shortages of food and the constant threats of punishment made against the community by the Japanese military administration, the option for a better life in Bahau must have indeed appeared promising at the time.

The Bahau initiative would live on as the darkest chapter in the lives of Singapore's tiny Eurasian community. And these scars still linger.

The follow pages offer a first-hand glimpse of the propaganda, misinformation and intimidation used by the Imperial Japanese Army during their brutal and repressive occupation of Singapore.

THE SYONAN TIMES – February 20 1942

DECLARATION
—OF THE—
COMMANDER OF THE NIPPON ARMY.

SINGAPORE is not only the connective point of the British Empire to control Britts-India, Australia and East Asia, but the strong base to invade and squeeze them and Britain has boasted of its impregnable features for many years and it is generally accepted as an unsurmountable fortress.

Since the Nippon armies, however, have taken a military operation on the Malay Peninsula and Singapore, they have overwhelmed the whole peninsula within only two months and smashed the strong fort to pieces within 7 days and thus the British dominating power in British India, Australia and East Asia has collapsed in a moment and changed in, as if, a fan without a rivet or an umbrella without a handle.

Originally, the English has entertained extremely egoistic and dogmatic principles and they not only have despised others, but have been accustomed to carry out the foxy, deceit, cunning and intimidation and they dared to commit the injustice and unrighteousness in order to keep only their own interest, and thus they have really spoiled the whole world.

Now, considering from the military proceeding of the Nippon Army and in view of the British administrations and their results, the traces of the British soldiers on Malayans are very clear and the British Armies during their operations and also on retreating from the front, have confiscated and looted the treasures, properties, provisions and reserves from the populace and cast them backward for destruction and dared to throw the people into slave point by burning their houses and also they placed the ladies and Australian troops on the front while the English troops remaining in Singapore, had the former at their back. Thus the English action, injustice and unrighteousness are beyond description and worthy to be called as the common enemy of humanity.

The reason why Nippon has stood up resolutely this time, taking her sword of evil-breaking, is very clear as already explained in several declarations of the Nippon Government and it is needless to declare again. We, however, hope that we sweep away the arrogant and unrighteous British elements and share pain and rejoicing with all concerned peoples in a spirit of "give and take," and also hope to promote the social development by establishing the East Asia Co-prosperity Sphere on which the New Order of Justice have to be attained under "the Great Spirit of Cosmocracy" giving all nations to its respective race and individual according to their talents and faculties. So, Nippon Army will hereafter endeavour further to sweep out the remaining power of Britain and U.S.A. from the adjoining regions and intend to realize the eternal development and policies of Malaya after curing the wound caused by British bloody squeeze in the long time past and restoring the war damage inflicted in this war.

Nippon armies hereby wish Malayan people to understand the real intention of Nippon and to co-operate with Nippon army toward the prompt establishment of the New Order and the Co-prosperity Sphere. Nippon army will drastically expel and punish those who still pursue needed dishonors as heretofore, those who indulge themselves in private interests and wants, those who act against humanity or disturb the public order and peace and those who are against the orders and disturb the military action of Nippon army.

On the fall of Singapore, the above declarations have hereby been given to the populace to indicate the right way for the purpose of eliminating their possible mistakes.

Tomoyuki Yamashita,
The Commander Of Nippon Army.

February, 2602.

Declaration of the Commander of the Nippon Army

Singapore is not only the connective pivot of the British Empire to control British India, Australia and East Asia, but the strong base to invade and squeeze them and Britain has boasted of its impregnable features for many years and it is generally accepted as an unsurmountable fortress.

Since the Nippon armies, however, have taken a military operation over the Malay Peninsula and Singapore, they have overwhelmed the whole peninsula within only two months and smashed the strong fort to pieces within 7 days and thus the British dominating power in British India, Australia and East Asia has collapsed in a moment and changed to, as if, a fan without a rivet or an umbrella without a handle.

Originally, the English has entertained extremely egotistic and dogmatic principles and they not only have despised others, but have been accustomed to carry out the foxy, deceit, cunning and intimidation and they dared to commit the injustice and unrighteousness in order to keep only their own interest, and thus they have really spoilt the whole world.

Now, considering from the military proceeding of the Nippon Army and in view of the British administrations and their results, the traces of the British squeeze on Malayans are very clear and the British Armies during their operations and also on retreating from the front, have confiscated and looted the treasures, properties, provisions and resources from the populace and sent them backward for destruction and dared to throw the people into severe pains by burning their houses and also they placed the Indian and Australian troops on the front while the English troops, remaining in Singapore had the former at their beck. Thus the English egotism, injustice and unrighteousness are beyond description and worthy to be called as the common enemy of humanity.

The reason why Nippon has stood up resolutely this time, taking her sword of evil-breaking, is very clear as already explained in the several declarations of the Nippon Government and it is needless to declare again. We, however, hope that we sweep away the arrogant and unrighteous British elements and share pain and rejoicing with all the concerned peoples in a spirit of "give and take," and also hope to promote the social development by establishing the East Asia Co-posterity Sphere on which the New Order of justice have to be attained under "the Great Spirit of Cosmocracy" giving all content to the respective race and individual according to their talents and faculties. So, Nippon Army will hereafter endeavour further to sweep out the remaining power of Britain and U.S.A. from the adjoining regions and intend to realise the eternal developments and policies of Malaya after curing the wound caused by the British bloody squeeze in the long time-past and restoring the war damage inflicted in this war.

Nippon armies hereby wish Malaya people to understand the real intention of Nippon and co-operate with Nippon army toward the prompt establishment of the New Order and the Co-prosperity Sphere. Nippon army will drastically expel and punish those who still pursue bended delusions as heretofore, those who indulge themselves in private interests and wants, those who act against humanity or disturb the public order and peace and those who are against these orders and disturb the military actions of Nippon army.

On the fall of Singapore, the above declarations have hereby been given to the populace to indicate the right way for the purpose of eliminating their possible mistakes.

Tomoyuki Yamashita
The Commander of Nippon Army
February, 2602

THE SYONAN TIMES – February 24 1942

Sword That Kills One & Saves Many!

IT has already been announced in the regular issues of this newspaper by the declaration of the Chief of the Syonan Defence Headquarters of the Nippon Army that severe punishment on the chief of the anti-Nipponese movement has been carried out. Henceforth the Nippon Defence Headquarters will punish all members of anti-Nippon movement whoever they may be. On the other hand the peace-loving citizens' daily businesses will be protected to the fullest extent.

Before the entrance of the Nipponese army into this island, Syonan (Singapore) was known throughout the world as a great British fortress in the Orient. Britain undoubtedly was the enemy of the Orient.

At the same time more than one half of the total population were composed of Chinese who secretly or publicly demonstrated sympathy and shook hands with the Chungking Government which

Sword that kills one & saves many!

It has already been announced in the regular issues of this newspaper by the declaration of the Chief of the Syonan Defence Headquarters of the Nippon Army that severe punishment on the chief of the anti-Nipponese

movement has been carried out. Henceforth the Nippon Defence Headquarters will punish all members of the anti-Nipponese movement whoever they may be. On the other hand the peace-loving citizens' daily businesses will be protected to the fullest extent.

Before the entrance of the Nipponese army into this island, Syonan (Singapore) was known throughout the world as a great British fortress in the Orient. Britain undoubtedly was the enemy of the Orient.

At the same time more than half of the local population were composed of Chinese who secretly or publicly demonstrated sympathy and shook hands with the Chungking Government which is the real enemy of Nippon. These Chinese who belonged to the last-mentioned category should not be considered as oriental people but as traitors of their own people. Many were forced to exhibit anti-Nipponese feelings and all Syonan was coloured by this feeling.

Divine Mercy

Old Singapore (now Syonan) boasted of the invincibility of its fortress. Oceans of ink were spilled to publicize its invincibility but within a week the Imperial Might of Nippon had smashed it like a match-wood construction. Britain has been proved to be rotten to the core.

All the people of Syonan who indulged in anti-Nipponese movement shaking hands with Britain and Chungking, and those who carried on espionage activities against Nippon or did actions to profit the enemies of Nippon should rightly be killed. However Nippon's divine mercy has been bestowed on them. Only those who disturb the peace of Syonan Island have been punished. The rest have been allowed to carry on with their daily business whatever it may be. This is a mercy which flows from the noble idea of the establishment of the Great East Asia Co-prosperity Sphere which again is based on the Great Nipponese Ideal of Cosmocracy. The Great Ideal of

Cosmocracy embraces all peace-loving men and does not embrace the men who disturb the establishment of the ideal against humanity.

The disturbers of the peace of the populace is a common enemy of all and will be killed by the Divine Sword. But the same sword which kills is also the saviour of thousands. This is the same Divine Sword that took the lives of traitors.

Those who want to stay in Syonan have promised to obey the orders and rule of the Nippon Army. It is indeed the duty of all inhabitants to obey the various orders and declarations issued by the Commander of the Nippon Army or by the Chief of the Syonan Defence Headquarters of the Nippon Army. Those who do not keep their promises of loyalty and continue to stir anti-Nipponese thoughts should be exposed to the Nipponese who will mete out just punishment to them.

Another word. It is not necessary only to do lip service to the cause of Nippon. Fear should not be the motive of adherence to the great and noble ideals of Nippon. You should obey the Nippon Army from the bottom of your heart. There must be a regeneration of thought to establish the Great East Asia Co-prosperity Sphere by Nippon. There must be positive co-operation for the establishment of the Great East Asian Cosmocracy! This is our message to you.

NOTE: This story alludes to Sook Ching massacre as it became known which saw up to 50,000 Chinese in Singapore slaughtered between February 18 and March 4 1942.

DECREE

IT is hereby decreed that all Eurasians must assemble at the Syonan Recreation Club ground (in front of the Municipal Building) at noon of 3rd March.

They should bring with them all particulars regarding Full Name (in Block Letters), Nationality, Age, Parentage, and former occupation. Those who have served as Volunteers or who have been in Government Service should state so clearly.

Food and water, to last for the duration of the Examination and Registration should also be brought.

By Order Of
THE COMMANDER OF THE NIPPONESE DEFENCE HEADQUARTERS.

THE SYONAN TIMES – March 4 1942

EURASIA ON THE PADANG
Community Must Face Realities

(By Charles Nell)

I WAS the witness to an amazing spectacle yesterday. It was the day appointed for the registration, by the Nippon Authorities, of the members of the Eurasian community of Syonan.

They rolled up in thousands, a few in motor cars, a few in rickshas, but the vast majority on foot until, that part of the esplanade, in front of the Syonan Recreation Club, set aside for the purpose, swarmed with them, like ants swarming around sugar.

But for a disgusting exhibition of lack of control, when the men tried to push themselves in with-

Eurasia on the Padang
Community must face realities

(By Charles Nell)

I was the witness to an amazing spectacle yesterday. It was the day appointed for the registration by the Nippon Authorities, of the members of the Eurasian community in Syonan.

The rolled up in their thousands, a few in motor cars, a few in rickshaws but the vast majority on foot, until that part of the esplanade, in front of the Syonan Recreational Club, set aside for the purpose swarmed with them, like ants swarming around sugar.

But for a disgusting exhibition of lack of control, when the men tried to push themselves in without the slightest consideration for the womenfolk, or for decent behaviour, which ended up in their being compelled to queue up and for some misunderstanding which led to large numbers going away without being registered, the business of registration passed off quietly and expeditiously with kindly and courteous treatment to all.

The amazing spectacle that I first referred to, however, was not their numbers or the varieties and combinations of races represented by this motley crowd. It was the eagerness with which the would-be European of British days strove to classify themselves as plain unvarnished Eurasians like their darker-hued brethren.

Whilst one has nothing but contempt for such avid turncoats, I am glad that they have come back to earth after their imaginary flights into the "heaven" created by the British for themselves and I must warn them that, today Malaya is ruled by a proud Asian Nation, the Nipponese, who will brook no attempts at any pro-British activities or tendencies.

Today we are Asians, free of British domination and the injustice and oppression which was part of their rule in the East, and any lingering hope that may lurk in the Eurasian breasts that the British will ever make a "Come-back" is but an idle and dangerous dream.

So, I would say to the Eurasians, never forget, even for a moment that it is your duty to co-operate fully and completely with the Nipponese authorities in their work of organizing the government of the country and of bringing about a return to the conditions of peace and co-prosperity for all.

You will have to go through difficult times, for the re-organization of any newly conquered country is a difficult task but if you will achieve a complete orientation of your mind and alter your outlook upon life and standards of living to suit such orientation, it will assist you through such difficult period.

Sincerity in your acceptance of an entirely Asian outlook, as subjects of a proud Asian Nation is the main factor needed. The principles underlining the great movement promulgated by the Nippon people for the creation of a New Order in East Asia, will provide you with the opportunity.

THE SYONAN TIMES – March 6 1942

NIPPONESE INJUNCTION TO LOCAL EURASIANS

Protection In Return For Faithful Co-operation

ADDRESSING members of the Eurasian community who had assembled on the padang outside the Syonan Recreation Club on Tuesday, the Chief of the Syonan Defence Headquarters declared:

The present Great Eastern War was started for the very existence of all Great Eastern peoples. We did not wish to start this war but under the circumstances we could not help it.

The Declaration of the Commander-in-Chief of the Nippon Army contains fully the object of this war. If any person interrupts our military actions in the least he will be severely punished. No one shall be allowed to act as an enemy of the Great Eastern peoples. But on the other hand people co-operating with us will be given every protection. They will suffer no hardships.

Until now you were spoiled in circumstances of individualism and liberalism. You were used to an easy-going life of amusements, but you will soon see the real idea of mankind, the new conception of the New World.

The 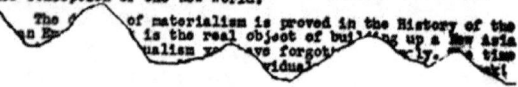 of materialism is proved in the History of the ... is the real object of building up a New Asia ...ualism ... ave forgot... ...ly. ...time

Nipponese injunction to local Eurasians
Protection in return for faithful co-operation

Addressing the members of the Eurasian community who had assembled on the padang outside the Syonan

Recreation Club on Tuesday, the Chief of Syonan Defence Headquarters declared:

> *The present Great Eastern War was started for the very existence of all Great Eastern peoples. We did not wish to start this war but under the circumstances we could not help it.*
> *The Declaration of the Commander-in-Chief of the Nippon Army contains fully the object of this war. If any person interrupts our military actions in the least he will be severely punished. No one will be allowed to act as an enemy of the Great Eastern peoples. But on the other hand people co-operating with us will be given every protection. They will suffer no hardships.*
> *Until now you were spoiled in circumstances of individualism and liberalism. You were used to an easy-going life of amusements, but you will soon see the real idea of mankind, the new conception of the New World.*
> *The defeat of materialism is proved in the History of the Roman Empire. It is the real object of building up a New Asia to gain the spiritualism you have forgotten entirely. The time for looking to personal and individual affairs is gone. Look! The burning of the dead lightens up the Syonan sky. The new dawn has come over a new Great Asia.*
> *Facing these facts some of you complained to us regarding small and petty personal affairs. This is regrettable. Most of you belong to the educated class and you still continue your thoughts and actions as before, disobeying our orders. We must think of a very heavy punishment for you.*
> *Those who emphasise their rights and ideas, forgetting their duties and services, are an evil to this nation. To anyone who persists in continuing to have old ideas, consistently disobeying our orders, we must consider meting out severe punishment.*

If you understand our true objective and serve Our Imperial Majesty, we shall take you up as new Japanese people – that we will accept you as our brothers.

THREE ORDERS

I demand of you obedience in the following three orders:

Those who served as Volunteers or in the Government Service such as in the Police or mischievous propaganda department shall state so clearly and in detail. If anyone is found to have given false information or having failed to comply with this order, he shall be severely punished.

Some military authorities are temporarily commandeering certain materials to facilitate military actions. Those who resist these authorities by refusing to allow an article to be commandeered, emphasising their ownership, act regrettably. This must not be so. Any person who is insolent to the Nippon Army shall be punished.

Those who were formerly employed in the Electrical, Water, Engineering and other important departments shall report at once to the Nippon Army to be reinstated in their jobs without delay. This must be done in order to speedily restore the various facilities of the city. Those who fail to do so shall be severely punished.

THE SYONAN SHIMBUN – December 7 1943

Catholics Allotted Land In Bahau For Development

NEWS WELCOMED WHOLEHEARTEDLY

"THE CATHOLIC Church has been allotted a block o agricultural lands at Bahau in Negri Sembilan, for a Catholic Colony," declared A. Devals, Bishop of Malacca, to a large gathering of Catholics at a meeting held at the Church of St. Peter and Paul on Sunday.

The thousands of Catholics residing in Syonan welcomed the news wholeheartedly and are eagerly awaiting for the day to peel off their shirts and start cultivating their plots with energy.

The Bishop further pointed out that the time had come for the people to change their occupation to that of labour or to undertake cultivation of land offered them.

"Syonan is now in great need for labourers and the whole population must be ready to give up all trades and undertake labour work. All unnecessary work now being done, for example, those of business class, or those who are not doing anything, must undertake the responsibility of earning their own living and produce necessary foodstu..." said Bishop.

Leader Urges Community To Make Best Of Offer

"WE HAVE been offered land for cultivation, and I call upon all Eurasians to take this opportunity and go back to the land," said Dr. C. J. Paglar leader of the Syonan Eurasians in an interview with the Syonan Sinbun.

Dr. Paglar declared that it was a glorious chance offered to his community, and it was up to every Eurasian to express his thanks to the Gunsei for considering such a small community as theirs in this gigantic plan.

"Everybody, not only Eurasians,..."

Catholics allotted land in Bahau for development
News welcomed wholeheartedly

"The Catholic Church has been allotted a block of agricultural land at Bahau in Negri Sembilan, for a Catholic Colony," declared A. Devals, Bishop of Malacca to a large gathering of Catholics held at the Church of St. Peter and Paul on Sunday.

Thousands of Catholics residing in Syonan welcomed the news wholeheartedly and are eagerly awaiting for the day to peel off their shirts and start cultivating their plots with energy.

The Bishop further pointed out that the time had come for the people to change their occupation to that of labour or to undertake cultivation of land offered to them.

"Syonan is now in great need for labourers and the whole population must be ready to give up all trades and undertake labour work. All unnecessary work now being done, for example, those of business class, or those who are not doing anything, must undertake the responsibility of earning their own living and produce necessary foodstuffs," said the Bishop.

It was also said that it was only for the working class of people that rice will be supplied. The lazy and the unemployed inhabitants, who do not want to work, and who consume rice, are depriving the labourers of the rice they need.

All facilities

The farming Catholic community to be started in Bahau, will have all religious facilities, churches, schools, convents, hospitals and the clergy. Land will be granted free at the rate of three acres of rice fields and two acres of jungle land per family.

Quarters, implements and other requirements for agricultural work will be supplied free by the Government till the families reach a stage where they can be self-supporting. Land and quarters are now ready for the would-be settlers and are ready to be occupied as soon as possible. Free transport will be provided.

The scheme is open to all Catholics including enemy aliens.

"This is a very good scheme," declared the Bishop "and I shall be very glad to give any advice put to me by any persons interested."

Catholics are asked to get in touch with their parish priests as soon as possible with regards to applying for enrolment.

Leader urges community to make best of offer
"We have been offered land for cultivation and I call upon all Eurasians to take this opportunity and go back to the land," said Dr. C. J. Paglar leader of the Syonan Eurasians in an interview with the Syonan Shimbun.

Dr. Paglar declared that it was a glorious chance offered to his community, and it up to every Eurasian to express his thanks to the Gunsel for considering such a small community as them in their gigantic plans.

"Everybody not just Eurasians, find that the Gunsel has mooted this scheme for the well being of the inhabitants," concluded the Eurasian leader.

NOTE: Bishop Devals died in Bahau following an injury to his foot which became infected. Dr. C. J. Paglar was arrested by the British on charges of treason after the war. He was put on trial in January 1946. However these charges were subsequently withdrawn. The Chief Welfare Officer of the Japanese Administration, Mamoru Shinozaki, testified on his behalf claiming that Paglar had acted under his direct instructions and that it was he who wrote the speeches for local community leaders during the Occupation years. In 1951 Dr. Paglar was elected as a member of the Legislative Council for Changi and he held this position until his death in 1954.

THE SYONAN SHIMBUN – *January 3 1944*

First Bahau settlers are elated

BAHAU, Dec 31 – Expressions of pleasant surprise were visible on the faces of the first batch of Catholic settlers from Syonan as they viewed their new settlement on their arrival here.

"How unlike the stuffy backlanes of congested Syonan," observed one as he inspected the barracks quartered. "My wife will be pleased with the romance of this rural scenery," declared another. "I feel elated at the opportunity offered to me to be one of the pioneers who will be responsible in helping Malai take the prodigious

step towards self-sufficiency in foodstuffs," philosophised a third. After thus expressing their individual impressions they voiced their determination to work hard and enhance the prosperity of the Colony.

The first batch of settlers consisted of 150 persons, mostly bachelors, were accompanied by M. Shinomaki. Kosei-ka Cho, Syonan Bishop Devals and some officials of the Gunselkan Bu, Syonan. Among them are carpenters, technicians, priests, medical men, anti-malaria experts, etc. Those men would put up country huts with the assistance of the Negri Sembilan Government, do anti-malarial work and install other necessary facilities so that their families and colleagues when they arrive may find the settlement comfortable. Further batches are expected on the 5th, 16th, 26th and 3rd of January and in February.

Amenities Provided
On their arrival the settlers after being entertained to tiffin were distributed with foodstuffs, mosquito nets, cigarettes, agricultural implements and household utensils.

Among the settlers who arrived and will arrive are, and will be, lawyers, doctors, teachers, etc. Those are coming here not because they are unhappy in Syonan but because they feel it is their duty to help the Administration in solving the foodstuff problem in Malai. As such this colony at Bahau is a striking instance of Catholic co-operation stated Mr. M. Shinomaki, when interviewed.

A member of the next batch, Mr. Shinomaki added, would be Mr. H. M. de Souza, Inspector of Schools, Syonan, who had resigned his post with the view of assisting the settlers. His wide knowledge of agriculture would be a great asset to the Colony, he explained. Mr. Shinomaki assured that settlers could look up to the Gunselkan Bu, Syonan, as a father who would provide them all assistance.

THE SYONAN SHIMBUN – January 3 1944

Catholics Eager To Go On The Land

WITH THE GUNSEIKAN'S words "Go, work hard and cultivate the land in determined fashion" still ringing in the ears of the first batch of Catholic pioneers who left Syonan for their settlement in Bahau recently, Syonan Catholics have been moved with but one desire, and that is, to go back to the land.

Catholics eager to go on the land

With the Gunseikan's words "Go, work hard and cultivate the land in determined fashion" still ringing in their ears, the first batch of Catholic pioneers who left Syonan for their settlement in Bahau recently, Syonan Catholics have been moved with but one desire and that is, to go back to the land.

Proud of their first batch of settlers, Catholics have been swung into action and are enrolling daily with their respective Parish priests and eagerly waiting their turn to entrain for their Colony which they are confident of turning their settlement into one big and successful food-producing garden. The Catholics most of whom being Chinese, Eurasians and Indians, are grateful to the authorities for meeting such a gigantic scheme which is in all ways to their favour, will exert every fibre of their being to prove their mettle by making their Colony sufficient in foodstuffs within the shortest time possible.

The site of the Colony is five miles from Bahau town, being situated in the Serting Hilir district, good roads have been systematically constructed or are in the course of construction so as to make transportation easy. Experts who formed an inspection party and recently visited the settlement returned with glowing reports of the Colony, declaring that it will turn out to be a little Paradise. The land is, at present, being irrigated by the Serting River, but construction work has now begun to further the irrigation of the settlement by diverting the Muar River to that area.

The Negri Sembilan Governor has promised the settlers all help and protection possible, and their self-administration will be as far as possible recognised by the authorities. Churches, schools, convents and the clergy will be at the disposal of the settlers while police stations, shops coffee stalls, places of amusement etc., will be run by the Catholics themselves.

Bahau seems to be the household word in every Catholic home and most of the would-be settlers have gone as far as to paint beautiful visions of what the settlement would look like in a few years to come. Catholics fully realise that there is a vast amount of arduous work ahead of them, and that it will not be a life of lolling around and watching their crops grow without the slightest effort of exertion.

On January 5 the second batch of Catholic pioneers are scheduled to leave for Bahau where they will join their friends and relatives of the first batch and cultivate the soil untiringly, awaiting for their comrades. Thus starts the building of a happy and peaceful settlement where every individual will play an important role towards the reconstruction of Malai.

THE SYONAN SHIMBUN – January 8 1944

Malaria unknown in Bahau, says medical practitioner

"Good land, pure water, beautiful surroundings and a healthy life will be the happy lot of those bound for their allotments in Bahau," declared Dr. M. Gaus, a leading Indonesian medical practitioner who recently visited Bahau with an inspection party comprising of Malais.

The Syonan Malai community has been allocated 4,500 acres of cleared land in Bahau for cultivation, thus enabling those Malais who are interested in farming and those who are at present idling or running little business establishments that are not benefiting them in the least to start a new life where every individual will be contributing his or her share towards the betterment of the country.

Said Dr. Gaus: "It's a glorious opportunity offered us, and I feel confident that Malais are eager to get back to the land. Our ancestors tilled the soil with brilliant success and I am sure that the present-day Malais will follow in their footsteps."

Dr. Gaus said that he found that there was very little trace of malaria in the settlement. He revealed that on making enquiries from the Chinese squatters who were already farming in the Bahau district, he found that many of them did not know what it was to suffer from malaria.

"A point which I wish to impress on the people of Syonan," said the Doctor, "is that Bahau is not an open piece of land with jungle all around it. It's just as lively and inhabited as Katong, Serangoon or any other district in Syonan." He went on to say that the town itself has good roads with brick houses. "Food is easily obtainable and at comparatively very low prices too," said the Doctor.

Dr. Gaus opined that the scheme has made a great impression on the Malais and that the people of his community are very grateful to the Gunsel for allotting them land in Bahau which will enable them to participate in the "Grow More Food Campaign".

Particularly, [word unclear] *...jawanese should prove their mettle in agricultural work," declared the Doctor, "as they are the people who have had long years of experience behind them."*

NOTE: In reality malaria, along with other tropical diseases, was endemic in Bahau resulting in the deaths of between 300 and 500 settlers.

THE SYONAN SHIMBUN – *January 10 1944*

Bahau Settlers working hard, determinedly, to make success of scheme
Considerable progress made

By Syonan Shimbun Staff Reporter

Fired with the idea of helping Malai to take a gigantic step towards food self-sufficiency are the pioneers of the Catholic settlement in Bahau. "The settlers are tackling the tasks allotted to them in a fast and determined manner," said Bishop Adrian Devals in an interview with the Syonan Shimbun on his return from Bahau recently.

He went on to say that the pioneers were hard at work with but one view, that being placing Malai on a food self-sufficiency basis. The scheme, said the Bishop, is receiving the unstinted and untiring support of the Gunsei, Negri Sembilan Government and the Kosei-ka Cho, who have the interest of the local inhabitants at heart.

The general public has the duty to perform, said the Bishop, of responding generously to the untiring efforts of the Gunsei, Negri Sembilan Government and the Kosei-ka Cho.

The Negri Sembilan Government makes a gift of a chankol (hoe) to every pioneer who sets foot on the settlement, the Bishop revealed. Seedling and cuttings are also supplied to the pioneers by the Government whenever needed.

Bishop Devals further added that the pioneers were now concentrating on agricultural work, and the building of homes and other necessary buildings. Said the Bishop: "The early batches have proved their mettle. They have made it possible for us to send up other batches of settlers according to plan."

He revealed that the first pioneers have played a large part by constructing or finishing housing accommodation for the settlers who have followed them. This proves that they are determined to work hard and enhance the prosperity of the settlement.

Stating that 141 families have already been allotted land, the Bishop said: "The first and second batches of pioneers are at present busying themselves erecting their homes on their own plots." The houses being built by the pioneers on their land are of simple construction.

All the houses are to be of uniform type, until such a time as the pioneers can find time to build better houses. Measuring 20 feet by 20 feet, the huts will have attap roofs and walls with a frame of wood poles. These huts, it is understood, are temporary and will later on be replaced by log cabins.

Barrack Houses
With the arrival of each new batch of settlers from Syonan, a further group of settlers are given land, said the Bishop, so that there will always be accommodation in the barracks for the new settlers to come. At the moment there are four barrack houses. Two are for the marrieds and the other two are for the bachelors. Cooking is done on a large-scale system. This will of course stop once the families move to their own plots.

That once the scheme is a success nothing will come up to it, is the confidence expressed by every Catholic. They know that life on a bed of roses does not await them in Bahau, and that there will be many hardships to endure, but they know that those hardships are not insurmountable.

All settlers will exert every fire in their beings to make the scheme a success. Some of them have already gone up and have written to friends and relatives stating that it's a life worth living – good land, pure air, and crystal-clear water that's Bahau.

Meanwhile non-Catholics who have not yet registered or who intend changing their occupations to that of a farmer in the Catholic Settlement in Bahau, are asked to get in touch with the various centres for enrolment forms.

The pioneers are at present receiving newspapers from Syonan thus enabling them to keep up with the current news.

Dr. C. J. Paglar, leader of the Syonan Eurasians revealed that the football presented to the pioneers in Bahau as a gift from the Syonan Shimbun had already been sent to them. He said the gift will help to encourage true sportsmanship amongst the settlers.

Bahau Catholic Settlement is fast developing into an ideal agricultural centre and a model settlement. When success is achieved, every settler will be the proud owner of a plot of flourishing land with a house of his own on it and will have the satisfaction of knowing that he or she has played an important role in the reconstruction of Malai.

THE SYONAN SHIMBUN – January 15 1944

Eurasians – Bahau calling!

The Bahau settlement scheme particularly in regard to its application to members of the Eurasian community in Syonan is something which all Eurasians who are fit and strong enough to go on the land should avail themselves of enthusiastically. Quite a number of suitable pioneers have already left for the site and others are awaiting their turn, but there is unlimited room at Bahau and those who have not yet registered their names are urged to do so in order that the authorities who are anxious to render this community every assistance in "getting on its feet' in healthy surroundings, may be convinced that Eurasians are worthy of the interest being taken in their welfare.

Never has any community, in any country been made such an offer – free land, free house, free provisions to tide over the initial period and food with pay during the collective work period in getting the sites ready for their families who will also be provided with allowances during the time the menfolk are initially engaged on this preliminary work! It is a stupendous offer and should be fully appreciated by those who stand to benefit by it.

A bright future faces the community. Instead of languishing in cities and growing steadily poorer, like the Portuguese of Malacca were allowed to under the British regime, all Eurasians whether they have the means or not have the opportunity of going on the land today and of making gentlemen farmers of themselves. A strong farming community forms the backbone of any country and Eurasians by availing themselves of this scheme, will be making themselves as economic asset to the country instead of continuing to be a liability, as they were under the old order, when they had no future as a community.

And what is perhaps most important at present, they will be showing a readiness to help the war effort by going to Bahau now: by joining with other farming communities towards the country's food needs when their families start producing. In addition to growing foodstuffs which they will find will spring up much more vigorously than possible on the island because the soil in Bahau is far richer, they will be able to raise chickens, ducks, pigs and goats. Some of them will find it profitable to establish dairy farms also. The opportunities at Bahau will be unlimited. This is their big chance!

THE SYONAN SHIMBUN – January 27 1944

Efforts Being Focussed On Food-Producing Plans At Endau, Bahau

BY SYONAN SHIMBUN REPORTER

THE STORY of Endau and Bahau is the tale of a grain of rice and the gigantic task that its production involves. The concentrated efforts of many officials and thousands of labourers and the speed at which this drive to attain self-sufficiency is being pushed through, merits its being termed, "Malai's blitzkreig food production."

A Prize For Every 10 Lottery Tickets: Official Statement

MANY new and attractive features will be introduced with the tenth issue of the Konan Saiken (Lottery) tickets which will [...] on [...] from Feb [...]

Endau and Bahau are more than just make-shift schemes by the authorities to create temporary food producing centres that intended to offset the present stoppage or difficulties experienced in the importation of foodstuffs, particularly rice.

What is known of Endau and Bahau is only the small beginnings of a gigantic scheme to convert millions of acres of the Malaian [...]

Efforts being focused on food-producing plans in Endau, Bahau

By Syonan Shimbun Reporter

The story of Endau and Bahau is a tale of grain and rice and the gigantic task that its production involves. The concentrated efforts of many officials and thousands of labourers and the speed at which this drive to attain self-sufficiency is being pushed through merits it being termed "Malal's blitzkrieg food production"

Endau and Bahau are more than just make-shift schemes by the authorities to create temporary food-producing centres that intend to off-set the present stoppage or difficulties experienced in the importation of foodstuffs, particularly rice.

What is known of Endau and Bahau is only the small beginnings of a gigantic scheme to convert millions of acres of the Malaian hinterland into food-producing areas that will, in the not too distant future, not only meet all of Malai's demands for foodstuffs but will place this country in the position of being able to export foodstuffs in addition to her other more widely known products.

The far-sighted among the local inhabitants are already aware of the beneficial influence these schemes will have on the physical, material, economic, cultural and political life of Malaians, and welcome the schemes and all they imply heartedly.

Country-wide development and land-settlement schemes that have already been floated have stepped up rice production in Malai well above the pre-war figure of 800,000 tonnes annually. The initial settlement schemes of Endau and Bahau, 2,400 acres in Endau and 3,000 acres in Bahau will enhance Syonan's position with regard to foodstuffs.

Bolstering Syonan's food position is the encouragement given to cattle-raising, poultry and pig-rearing and vegetable gardening by both the Gunseikan-bu and the Tokubatu-si in regard to the fixation of prices to suit the pockets of farmers and gardeners. Similar encouragement is given to the Provincial Governments with the objective of achieving self-sufficiency in foodstuffs within the shortest time possible.

The amount of time and effort that the authorities are devoting to the development of these schemes shows the importance that the Government attaches to them. They are, at any rate, very important to every Malaian because they vitally concern every man, woman and child in the country. It is for this reason that those charged with the realization of Endau and Bahau, call for and are receiving the co-operation of the people of Syonan.

THE SYONAN SHIMBUN – February 28 1944

SYOWA 19

Bahau, New Syonan Settlers Fast Getting Into Their Stride

WILL STOP AT NOTHING IN BID TO ATTAIN SELF-SUFFICIENCY IN FOOD

BY SYONAN SHIMBUN STAFF REPORTER

WHAT struck him most was the determined spirit of the settlers in New Syonan and Bahau to let nothing stop them from carrying the food self-sufficiency scheme there to fruition within the least possible time, said Mr. Lim Chong Pang, vice-chairman of the Propaganda Department of the Overseas-Chinese Association, in an interview with the Syonan Shimbun on his return from a tour of New Syonan and Bahau.

"Everybody in New Syonan and Bahau," said Mr. Lim, "is toiling hard from dawn till dusk daily, helping to clear up the land and to carry out such work as there is to be done."

"And believe me," added Mr. Lim, "there is a lot of work to be done. The point I must emphasise is that the work is being done well."

"Rich or poor, young or old, everybody is doing work," said Mr. Lim. "The old are given light work; the able-bodied hard work; but rich and poor alike, all have work to do." As a matter of interest, the oldest settler in Bahau is 81 years of age; the youngest only a month old.

So much work is being accomplished both at New Syonan and Bahau, that in a few months there will be great change, said Mr. Lim.

HEALTHY SURROUNDINGS

Hard work and healthy surroundings are making New Syonan and Bahau settlers sturdy men and women. The men are sun-tanned and muscular, while men, women and children have a ... red ... cheerful hope ul, con...

In Bahau, mosquito-nets made of pineapple leaf fibre are being used.

It is believed that two doctors will be proceeding from Syonan to Bahau in the near future.

"The settlers both in New Syonan and Bahau are all grateful to the Kosei-ka Cho for all that he has done for them," said Mr. Lim. "To the children as well as the grown-ups, the Kosei-ka Cho is like a Santa Claus.... whenever he goes up to Bahau and New Syonan, the Kosei-ka Cho takes with him cigarettes, sweets and other presents which are greatly appreciated. The settlers always look forward to a visit from the Kosei-ka Cho.

GRATITUDE TO KOSEIKA CHO

When he thanked them for coming to help in the development of New Syonan and Bahau, the latest batch of settlers who arrived there said they owed the opportunity to the Kosei-ka Cho whose help and understanding had made it possible for them to migrate to New Syonan and Bahau where a glorious future awaited them.

The 46 Po Leung Kuk girls who recently arrived at New Syonan are already doing useful work. They ...

Bahau, New Syonan settlers fast getting into their stride
Will stop at nothing in bed to attain self-sufficiency in food

By Syonan Shimbun Staff Reporter

What struck him most was the determined spirit of the settlers in New Syonan and Bahau to let nothing stop them from carrying the food self-sufficiency scheme there to fruition within the least possible time, said Mr Lim Chong Pang, vice-chairman of the Propaganda Department of the Overseas Chinese Association in an interview with the Syonan Shimbun on his return from a tour of New Syonan and Bahau.

"Everybody in New Syonan and Bahau," said Mr Lim, "is toiling hard from dawn to dusk daily, helping to clear up the land and to carry out such work as there is to be done."

"And believe me," added Mr Lim, "there is a lot of work to be done. The point I must emphasize is that the work is being done well."

"Rich or poor, young or old, everybody is doing work," said Mr Lim. "The old are given light work; the able-bodied hard work, but rich and poor alike, all have work to do." As a matter of interest, the oldest settler in Bahau is 81 years of age; the youngest only one month old.

"So much work is being accomplished both at New Syonan and Bahau that in a new months there will be a great change," said Mr Lim.

Healthy Surroundings
Hard work and healthy surroundings are making New Syonan and Bahau settlers sturdy men and women. The

men are sun-tanned and muscular while men, women and children acquired a cheerful, hopeful, contented outlook.

He mentioned that among the last batch of settlers who arrived at New Syonan were millionaires-businessmen proprietors (and their whole families) of such big firms as Kwong Fook Tai, Pue Tai Cheong, Sun Cheong, Cheong Lee Yuen, Yick Tai and many others.

Considerable hard work lies before these millionaire-businessmen and their families and it is with full knowledge of this fact that they have gone to New Syonan, determined to help in the gigantic food self-sufficiency drive.

The latest batch of Bahau settlers consisting of about 240 Chinese Roman Catholics who left Syonan on Feb 20 were taken by train right up to their doorsteps. The train halted right by their settlement and the settlers went to their new home right from the railway carriage.

It is stated that the train will in the future make bi-weekly halts at this point to serve the convenience of the settlers. Indicative of the interest taken by the authorities is the fact that this batch of settlers were accompanied to their settlement by the Keizai-bu Cho and other officials.

While at Bahau Mr. Lim gathered that already 320 families had been allotted an area of three acres each and that their respective houses are fast taking shape now.

Bishop Devals

Mr Lim praised Bishop Devals and his assistant for their untiring and unselfish work in Bahau. Their example is an inspiration to the settlers there.

Site for a post office and hospital are being prepared next to the police station at Bahau. At present postal service is maintained three times a week.

The use of substitute materials is speeding up considerably the construction of houses for the settlers at

Bahau said Mr Lim who suggested that this step be followed in New Syonan.

In Bahau Mr Lim related that attap for roofing purposes is being replaced by certain species of ferns known as 'puchet' and the leaves of palm trees known as 'palas' which serve the purpose just as well, and he thinks that the completion of houses in New Syonan need not be delayed by the lack of attap.

The sawmill sent to Endau some time ago has started operations and this, said Mr Lim, will result in speeding up the completion of houses for the New Syonan settlers.

The framework of numerous houses is already standing and it only remains for the roof, outer walls and partitions and bedding platforms to be completed. The bark of trees is being used in place of planks for the outer walls in some cases.

An important departure from the original policy concerning New Syonan was disclosed by the Kosei-Ka Cho, Mr. M. Shinozaki, in the course of discussion at New Syonan recently.

Other business also

The Kosei-Ka Cho said it had now been decided to allow Chinese to migrate to New Syonan to start any legitimate businesses of their own choosing because it was felt that this would encourage people to open businesses there thus accelerating the settlement of families and the development of New Syonan. For the time being, no licences are necessary and there will be no restrictions of any kind.

"If the pioneers of the New Syonan find that it is possible to be rewarded through businesses in addition to their yield from their allotment, then by all means let them engage in businesses," said Mr. Shinozaki. "For being pioneers, they deserve to be rewarded."

"If people come here to prosper, then let us welcome them to New Syonan."

The health of settlers both in New Syonan and Bahau is being maintained. In Bahau mosquito nets made of pineapple leaf fibre are being used. It is believed that two doctors from Syonan will go to Bahau in the near future.

"The settlers both in New Syonan and Bahau are very grateful to the Kosei-Ka Cho for all that he has done for them," said Mr. Lim. "To the children as well as the grown-ups, the Kosei-Ka Cho is like a Santa Claus ... whenever he goes up to Bahau or New Syonan, the Kosei-Ka Cho takes with cigarettes and sweets and other presents which are greatly appreciated." The settlers always look forward to a visit by the Kosei-Ka Cho.

Gratitude to the Kosei-Ka Cho

When he thanked them for coming to help in the development of the New Syonan and Bahau, the latest batch of settlers who arrived said they owed the opportunity to the Kosei-Ka Cho whose help and understanding made it possible for them to migrate to New Syonan and Bahau where a glorious future awaited them.

"After my tour of New Syonan and Bahau, I feel that no one who is anxious to improve his prospects and insure his future should hesitate to migrate to these settlements, unless of course he is doing essential work," said Mr. Lim

Mr. Lim added that among the settlers at New Syonan and Bahau are many businessmen and clerks who realise that in the New Syonan and Bahau they have definitely a more promising future.

A NOTE FROM THE AUTHOR

In October 2009 while working at the National Heritage Board, I wrote a series of blog posts about the war in Singapore. This is an extract from one entitled: *Fantasies of the Unconscious – Fire in the Sky:*

I'm sure I had been told the story before … probably years ago but it was since forgotten. The subject came up purely by chance a few weeks back during one of my long-overdue visits to my mother's place.

"I'm going to visit the Kranji War Memorial next week – it's just work," I announced. Well up to that point it was a rather dull conversation so even an intended visit to a graveyard had an edge of uplifting excitement.

"Don't forget to visit your grandfather," she intoned.

"Huh?" was my reply.

Mum rolls her eyes to heaven (yeah sarcasm runs deep in the family) … and so the story was retold.

My maternal grandfather Arthur Henry Nunes died many years earlier during the Japanese Occupation of Singapore.

Word had gone out in the middle of 1941 asking for civilian volunteers. Help was needed for civil defence both to direct people to air-raid shelters, and for putting out the fires from the aerial bombs that everyone knew were surely to come. Others were asked to join the Local

Defence Corps – essentially to help out with the military defence of the island.

The Singapore Free Press

WEDNESDAY, JUNE 11, 1941.

Eurasian Volunteers

THE appeal which has been issued for more recruits for the Eurasian companies of the Singapore Volunteers Corps deserves the immediate attention and full support of the community. In the eighty odd years since the formation of the Corps, the Eurasian community of this city has made important contributions to the life and work of the Corps and the Eurasian sub-units have splendid records of service of which they may well be proud. To-day, at a time when the Empire is facing the gravest crisis in its long history, it is fitting that Eurasians should be playing a full part in the responsible war role that has been allotted to the Corps, but if the Eurasian sub-units are to perform their tasks

The latter was considered more dangerous but also more prestigious – probably because you would be armed with a rifle and would soon be in the thick of the action. So being a young man, my grandfather like many other Eurasians of his generation, opted for the military.

My mother, who would have been about 14 at the time I guess, couldn't quite remember the details apart from the fact that her father was a rather eccentric individual with a volcanic temper (traits I was destined to inherit).

Seeing the Japanese planes bombing Singapore at will without a thought for the innocent civilians killed and maimed, must have ignited that anger which apparently knew no bounds.

"He used to run around pointing his rifle in the sky, taking pot-shots at the planes" she said.

Of course he never hit anything. The Japanese fighters and even the bombers were probably flying too high and going too fast but I guess he wanted to make a statement – that we – or at least he – would not go down without a fight.

He survived the invasion but died during the Occupation of tuberculosis at the age of just 43.

And so when I finally made it to the Kranji War Memorial a week later, I headed straight to locate the memorial to a man I owe my life to (in a way) but never knew 'cept in some old faded photographs.

Among the many columns dedicated to Allied soldiers who gave their all for Singapore, I found the wall listing the names of our local volunteers. And there, high above my head and carved in cold ageless stone was his name – 'Nunes A. H.'

I stood there for several minutes waiting to feel well ... something. I had envisioned that it would be a special, humbling moment of sorts ... stretching across time and space to be reunited for a moment with a family member long gone.

And so I waited as sweat trickled down my face but there were no harps playing gently in the background nor was there a chorus of angels.

Damn … nothing happened. I felt a little cheated.

It should have been something grand, unforgettable but all I felt was the heat of the noon-day sun. I took a photograph just to show I was there, turned and walked away.

I still didn't know him any better. It was just another name on a wall, one name among thousands, nothing more.

As I headed down the gently sloping grounds to the bus, a group of people were laying a wreath of poppies. I stopped in respect and watched as a styrofoam wreath covered with tacky plastic poppies was placed against a Christian cross bearing a long sword in the centre.

At this point I wasn't looking to feel anything and so I wasn't disappointed.

Walking on as I passed row upon row of white tombstones, the utter futility of this hallowed ground sank in. So and So aged 23 – Dead, So and So aged 19 – Dead, Unknown Soldier – Dead. Was it worth it? Singapore had been billed as an impenetrable fortress and yet we didn't even put up much of a fight, surrendering in about a week.

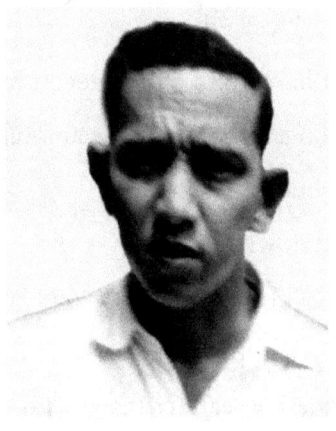

So maybe that crazy guy who pointed his rifle at the red devils of the rising sun as they flew on towards the city to unleash yet another load of wanton destruction and fired round after round until his magazine of his weapon clicked empty, wasn't that mad after all.

When all seems lost and hope has run cold, in a time of madness maybe the only sane thing left to do is to fire your weapon into the sky in one last act of defiance for freedom, for country … and for family.

    Rest well A. H. Nunes. To be honest, I still don't know you but I'm walking away with a sense of pride. I think I'm beginning to understand ...

ABOUT THE AUTHOR

David Miller worked as a police investigator in Singapore before starting his writing career first as a newspaper correspondent and later as a managing editor for a stable of magazines.

Over the years he has written a number of commercial books for both the public and private sectors.

His first novel *Year of the Tiger* was printed in August 2012. *Advent* was published in June 2013 and he is currently working on his third book to complete the series. *Bahau, the Elephant & the Ham* and *DutyBound* were published in November 2014.

For more about the author, visit his website at www.dmbooks.org

A WORD OF THANKS

I am deeply grateful to Jan Tristram and Karen Pittock for their invaluable help in the production of this book. Readers, if you enjoyed reading ***Bahau, the Elephant & the Ham***, please spend a few minutes penning your thoughts in a review at your favourite book retailer. Your comments are most appreciated.

If you prefer to contact me directly with your comments, please email *feedback@dmbooks.org*

Cheers,
David

OTHER BOOKS BY DAVID MILLER

YEAR OF THE TIGER

A WARTIME SECRET IN SINGAPORE TRIGGERS A GLOBAL BIOTERRORISM NIGHTMARE

During World War II, the Imperial Japanese Army under General Tomoyuki Yamashita looted untold amounts of gold and other valuables from across its occupied colonies in Southeast Asia to finance the empire's on-going military expansion.

But when the tides of war turned against Japan in 1943, much of this treasure had to be buried in secret. Over the decades, the search for the legendary Yamashita's Gold had been in vain until now...

A group of foreign workers digging a tunnel under the Padang in present-day Singapore stumbles across a treasure vault and inadvertently triggers a biological booby trap. An unknown strain of anthrax is released threatening a global holocaust. It is up to investigators in Singapore to decipher a cryptic clue left behind with the loot and halt this deadly plague.

Year of the Tiger
ISBN (Paperback) 978-981-4358-89-7
ISBN (Ebook) 978-981-4358-90-3
www.dmbooks.org

ADVENT
THE COUNTDOWN HAS BEGUN

From the deadly attacks on US embassies in Africa to the Bali bombings to 9-11 – these have left the world reeling in shock and fear. Horrific as these bloody terrorist operations were, they were in essence nothing more than just random strikes without any real long-term agenda.

But what if lurking in the shadows now was an even more sinister force – one intent on world domination at any cost. Following a script almost as old as time itself, it would put religion and politics on an inevitable collision course blurring forever the lines of good and evil.

From Washington, to Jerusalem's sacred Temple Mount to the hallowed halls of the Vatican, the final struggle for global conquest has been set in motion – the advent to Judgement Day is upon us.

Advent
ISBN (Paperback) 978-981-07-6390-9
ISBN (Ebook) 978-981-07-6389-3
www.dmbooks.org

DUTYBOUND
A SINGAPORE WAR HERO REMEMBERED

This is a true story of a young police inspector who finds himself out of a job during the Japanese Occupation of Singapore. He begins to fight back in his own way and is soon lured into joining a clandestine Allied spy ring.

Working in disguise, 22-year-old Halford Boudewyn is tasked to smuggle out classified documents from a POW camp which could prevent another major invasion planned by the Imperial Japanese Army.

This book is written based on the notes Boudewyn left behind shortly before his death. Now for the first time, his complete story can be told.

DutyBound
ISBN (Paperback) 978-981-09-2389-1
ISBN (Ebook) 978-981-09-2390-7
www.dmbooks.org